MW00611512

History of Greece

A Captivating Guide to Greek History, Starting from the Bronze Age in Ancient Greece Through the Classical and Hellenistic Period to the Modern Era

© Copyright 2021

All Rights Reserved. No part of this book may be reproduced in any form without permission in writing from the author. Reviewers may quote brief passages in reviews.

Disclaimer: No part of this publication may be reproduced or transmitted in any form or by any means, mechanical or electronic, including photocopying or recording, or by any information storage and retrieval system, or transmitted by email without permission in writing from the publisher.

While all attempts have been made to verify the information provided in this publication, neither the author nor the publisher assumes any responsibility for errors, omissions or contrary interpretations of the subject matter herein.

This book is for entertainment purposes only. The views expressed are those of the author alone, and should not be taken as expert instruction or commands. The reader is responsible for his or her own actions.

Adherence to all applicable laws and regulations, including international, federal, state and local laws governing professional licensing, business practices, advertising and all other aspects of doing business in the US, Canada, UK or any other jurisdiction is the sole responsibility of the purchaser or reader.

Neither the author nor the publisher assumes any responsibility or liability whatsoever on the behalf of the purchaser or reader of these materials. Any perceived slight of any individual or organization is purely unintentional.

Free Bonus from Captivating History (Available for a Limited time)

Hi History Lovers!

Now you have a chance to join our exclusive history list so you can get your first history ebook for free as well as discounts and a potential to get more history books for free! Simply visit the link below to join.

Captivatinghistory.com/ebook

Also, make sure to follow us on Facebook, Twitter and Youtube by searching for Captivating History.

Contents

Introduction: It's All Greek to Me

Greece stands large in the minds of many as the epic spawning ground of Western civilization. It was here that philosophy, democracy, science, mathematics, and just about everything else that the Western world might take for granted was forged. Most scholars agree that we owe much to the culture of ancient Greece. But as high as we hold the Greece of the bygone past, we have to realize that Greek history did not end in the era of Socrates, Plato, and Aristotle.

After the Classical era, Greek history merged and melded with the Roman Empire in what would later be termed the Greco-Roman period. Even though Rome conquered Greece and turned the once free Greek city-states into subjects of Rome, the Romans had great respect for this subject people. So much so, in fact, that they adopted their customs as their own. Greek philosophy, religion, sports, and theater are just a few aspects of Greek culture that the Romans sought to infuse with their own.

Even the Greek language became popular and was one of the most widely spoken languages of the Roman Empire, second to Latin. It was during this timeframe that a previously unknown sect of Judaism called Christianity would rise up to influence and then ultimately supersede Greek philosophy. The combination of Roman roads and a common Greek language were the greatest facilitators for the preaching of the gospel.

Rome did indeed come to accept Christianity, and eventually, it would become the dominant religion, with Roman Emperor Constantine establishing a new capital all the way in the Greek East—Constantinople. Under the backdrop of a Christianized Roman Empire, Greek power grew in the east until the eastern half of the Roman dominion was distinctly Greek in flavor.

The Western Roman Empire would fall in the meantime, while the eastern half continued under the Greek-speaking and Greek-thinking Byzantine Empire, which was based out of the Greek capital of Constantinople. This phase of Greek culture would last until it was toppled by the Ottoman Turks in 1453. Greece itself would then be controlled by the Ottoman Empire until it finally wrested its freedom from the Turks in 1821.

It has been a long struggle since then, and Greece has survived two world wars, a civil war, a military junta, an economic collapse, and a worldwide pandemic. Yes, there is much more to Greek history than just Socrates, Plato, and Aristotle. As important as classical Greece is, it is important not to forget the continuing saga of Greek culture. Here is the history of Greece in full.

Chapter 1 – The Origins of Ancient Greece

"Fables should be taught as fables, myths as myths, and miracles as poetic fantasies. To teach superstitions as truths is a most terrible thing. The child mind accepts and believes them, and only through great pain and perhaps tragedy can he be in after years relieved of them."

-Hypatia of Alexandria

The mists of time hang low over Greece at its inception. And there is no way of knowing exactly what prehistoric Greece might have been like. We do receive some pretty good hints, however, in the form of Greek mythology and plenty of anecdotal lore. These myths, of course, should be taken much as they are perceived—as myths. But even if they are fictitious renderings, they impart crucial details of what Greek life at the very dawn of human history must have been like.

The legends of old describe motivating factors for Greek society and imbue Greek culture with its own sense of manifest destiny. Although most are not likely to take, for example, the epic journey of Odysseus, literally, the indomitable spirit and courageous virtues portrayed within the tale would be a sounding board for future

Greek temperament. Greek researcher and writer Thomas R. Martin refers to this as the "concentration on excellence" displayed in the Greek imagination. The epic characters portrayed in these narratives represented the Greek ideal of what they longed for themselves and their society as a whole to achieve.

The *Odyssey* and the *Iliad* come down to us from the so-called Archaic period of Greece as tales that were passed down orally, meaning they were spoken or sang in front of an audience. The *Iliad* actually takes place before the *Odyssey* and revolves around the Trojan War. The *Odyssey*, on the other hand, occurs after the events of the *Iliad*. The tale of heroic Odysseus, who returned home after an absence of twenty years, would have been particularly stirring to Greek ears. And the fact that his wife Penelope had remained faithful to him after all of those years would have elicited reactions of admiration for her loyalty and dedication.

Besides these echoes of the primordial past, the real spark began when the Greeks first learned to express themselves in the written word. The Greeks are believed to have reached this epoch around 770 BCE, for it was at this time that the Greeks first began to record their own history.

Prior to this, much of what prehistoric Greece was like is largely unknown. Even once the Greeks started to write things down, it took a while for the ancient Greeks to become prolific writers. With this deluge of material, it can be hard to separate legend from reality, but one must at least try to discern the difference, for even the fabrications tell us a little something about the mentality of ancient Greek civilization.

One thing that is certain is that the early Greeks were a people fixated on those who came before them. Today, folks who are interested in their ancestors might go to an ancestry website, look up their family tree, and leave it at that. Such things are perhaps just a passing curiosity—nothing more and nothing less. Back in the days of ancient Greece, however, who came before you could mean just about everything.

From potentates to the average citizen, groups of early Greeks categorized themselves based upon their lineage from a powerful figure from the past. These descendants were often the heroes and, in some cases, even the demigods of legendary lore. It was through this lineage that the Greeks declared themselves to be the progeny of greatness. The most popular of these patron patriarchs is that of Hellen.

Although those of us in the West are more familiar with Hellen (or rather Helen) being used as a feminine moniker, the Hellen of ancient Greek lore was the bold son of Deucalion, who, in turn, is the son of the Greek Titan Prometheus. In Greek mythology, the Titans were a class of celestial beings who ended up waging war against the Greek gods of Olympus, otherwise known as the "Olympians."

As Greek myth tells us, the Olympians ultimately won in this struggle, and the Titans were defeated. However, two of those Titans, Prometheus and his brother Epimetheus, had remained neutral during the conflict, so they managed to escape punishment. After the war was over, in fact, they were recruited by the head honcho of the Olympians, Zeus, to do a bit of divine work on Earth.

According to legend, the Titan Epimetheus was tasked with designing all of the animal life on Earth. His brother Prometheus, in the meantime, was given the special assignment of creating an intelligent lifeform to reign at the top of the food chain: human beings. It is said that Prometheus formed human beings from the very mud and muck of the earth. And since all of the baser biological attributes, such as sharp teeth, claws, and shells, were given to the animals for defense and offense, Prometheus had to contemplate an alternative means of giving this higher lifeform distinction over the other creations.

He determined to create these beings as nothing short of the very "image" of the gods. For anyone familiar with the Book of Genesis in the Bible, you might be a little stunned at the similarity. Here we have two creation stories that speak of human beings being made of the "dust" of the earth and also made in the "image" of the divine. As to what "image" might mean, though, has long been debated. Some take it as a literal interpretation that humanity was made to have a similar appearance to divine beings. Others who wish to delve deeper into the metaphysics of it all theorize that the legend is referring to the human soul being imaged to the mortal clay of the human form. Just like a computer is "imaged" with data, Prometheus sparked within us a divine program of sorts—or at least so this myth would have us believe.

At any rate, according to Greek myth, shortly after Prometheus forged man, he began to pity him. Despite their divine software, physically speaking, human beings just seemed too weak and defenseless to hold their own in the world. As such, Prometheus wanted to give humanity something that would give them an edge. Even though it was not permitted, Prometheus decided to intervene on man's behalf by giving them the gift of fire.

Another interesting parallel from Judeo-Christianity is the extra-biblical narrative found in the Book of Enoch, which claims that fallen angels transgressed against God by teaching human beings certain arts that God felt they were not ready for. In Greek myth, the Titan Prometheus is said to be playing a very similar role. He was trying to aid humanity, but he broke a prime directive in doing so.

And according to Greek legend, Prometheus paid a terrible price for going against Zeus's orders. He is said to have been stretched out against a rock and chained in place so that a giant bird of prey could peck at him (in particular, at his liver) for all of eternity. Sounds like a pretty terrible fate by any stretch of the imagination.

At any rate, it was Prometheus's son Deucalion who supposedly fathered Hellen with his wife, Pyrrha. Interestingly enough, Deucalion is sometimes known as the Greek "Noah" because the myth surrounding Deucalion is a flood story, very much reminiscent of the one in the biblical Book of Genesis. In this account, Zeus is angry and disgusted with the depravity of humans and orchestrates a flood to wipe them off the face of the earth. However, Deucalion was warned of what would happen, and taking refuge in a giant "wooden chest," he and his family survived the deluge.

Deucalion's son Hellen is said to have given rise to the first Greeks through his sons Aeolus, Dorus, and Xuthus. Greek ancestry is said to have split between these three sons, giving rise to the Aeolians, Dorians, and, by way of the two sons of Xuthus— Achaeus and Ion—the Achaeans and Ionians. It was these four main tribes, which were ultimately descended from Hellen, that were said to make up the Hellenes of the ancient Greeks.

Another major part of ancient Greek tradition was to create incredible backstories to certain geographic locales. In the region of Greece known as "Hellas," for example, it is said that Hellen himself resided there as a king in the shadow of Mount Othrys in Thessaly. According to the mythological backstory, when Hellen's reign came to a close, he was replaced by his heir, Aeolus. It was then the children of Aeolus who ended up spreading out from Thessaly to form a greater Greece that stretched all the way to Corinth in the south and Peloponnesus in the west. This branch of Hellenes was said to have traveled far and wide as they populated the far reaches of ancient Hellas (Greece).

Those who are said to have hailed from the Achaean branch played a major role in the so-called "Heroic Age," in which they perfected the art of war in Sparta, Argos, and Mycenae. They were the stars of the great Trojan War, a tale of which it has only recently been discovered must contain some kernels of truth in the midst of all of its grand myth-making.

The Trojan War, you see, revolved around the city of Troy. Troy was long believed to be entirely fictional, but excavations on the western shores of modern-day Turkey have revealed a city that seems to have been the mythical backdrop of this epic struggle, with several Greek artifacts unearthed from the time period in question. At any rate, it was the Achaeans who fought in the Trojan War who filled up much of ancient Greece's lore, with the blind poet Homer often calling the sum total of the Greek population simply "Achaeans."

The Ionians and Dorians, in the meantime, initially played a lesser role in ancient Greece, but eventually, they would come to take center stage by helping to give rise to both the Athenians and Spartans, the latter of which are perhaps the most famous military arm of the Greeks. For the Spartans, martial defense was everything, and people were recruited and trained to fight in the Spartan armed forces as young as seven years old.

Today, the notion of a child soldier would be complete anathema to most of us. But for the Spartans, fighting was simply a way of life, and they taught their youth that they had to learn the skills of warfare from a young age. Even infants were not immune to this critique since it wasn't uncommon for newborn children to be left to die if they were deemed to be somehow deficient and therefore not suitable to grow up to be a fighter. Again, such things today would be absolutely abhorrent from a modern perspective, but for the Spartans, such drastic measures were just part of who they were as a people.

The Spartans eventually clashed with the Athenians in the 5th century BCE, besting their foes around 404 BCE in what was known as the Peloponnesian War. As fiery as their spirits were, the Spartans' decline began to set in by 370 BCE after the Spartans lost out to another Greek group called the Thebans. And since the Spartans did not leave much of cultural value other than their art of war, their actual influence on the shape of Hellenization can be said to be fairly minimal.

The most enduring bond of any nation, of course, is its language. So, where did the Greek language come from? This question by itself opens up the door of yet another fascinating facet of not only Greek but also world history as a whole. Historians have traced the Greek language back to a large, mysterious people group from the distant past referred to as the Indo-Europeans.

The Indo-Europeans were said to have originated somewhere in Eurasia before swooping down on lands as far afield as Greece, Iran, and even India (hence Indo-European). It is said that the first wave of Indo-Europeans arrived during the Early and Middle Helladic periods around 2000 BCE. The fact that these Indo-Europeans were most likely not on a mission of peace is evident by the archaeological record, which seems to bear witness to the sudden destruction and dislocation of those who were already in the region upon the arrival of the Indo-Europeans.

If groups were not altogether pushed out, they seem to have intermingled and eventually intermarried with the newcomers. It seems that the Greek language as we know it today was forged in this cultural melding of the Indo-Europeans and the older inhabitants who had crossed paths with them thousands of years ago. The Greeks themselves referred to the original peoples who lived in Greece in the primordial past as being the "Pelasgians." Not all of the Pelasgians lost their original identity, and some pockets are said to remain in Attica and Arcadia.

At any rate, it was during the Middle Helladic period, around 1600 BCE, that the majority of Greek and Indo-European descendants began to create a complex civilization, complete with citadels, temples, and palaces. Since much of this civilization is found in the southern Greek city of Mycenae, this ancient Greek society is often called Mycenaean.

According to Greek myth, Mycenae served as the backdrop of the killing of the Mycenean King Agamemnon at the hands of his wife, Clytemnestra. During the Trojan War, King Agamemnon came back with the spoils of war, which just so happened to include a certain Trojan priestess named Cassandra (also spelled as Kassandra). Agamemnon's wife was apparently not too happy about all this. She was unhappy enough, in fact, that she conspired to have her husband killed.

Although this story is generally viewed as the product of myth-making, there are those who have tried to argue that perhaps at least some of this tale is true. A researcher by the name of Heinrich Schliemann, in fact, even claimed to have found the burial site of this long-dead Mycenean king, a site full of buried artifacts and even a "golden death mask." But subsequent inquiries into this archaeological find revealed none of the artifacts were from the time period in which King Agamemnon is said to have lived. So it is that the veracity of this tale remains a mystery.

The very real footprints of the Mycenean civilization, however, remain clearly distinct, with outposts stretching to Athens and Thebes. The Myceneans were also the first Greeks to develop writing, coming up with what is known as Linear B around 1000 BCE.

Before the rise of epic Greek literature, most of these early writings contain notes of everyday life, such as the listings of foodstuffs and the like. Although the Myceneans had the Indo-Europeans as ancestors, they were clearly influenced by their Near Eastern neighbors, such as the nearby Minoans of Crete. Artwork, pottery, and other sculptures that have been recovered show a deep similarity between the two cultures. Much of this influence most likely came from seaborn commerce between the two regions.

As rapidly as the Myceneans had risen, their downfall was even faster. It seems that around 1200 BCE, the whole civilization faced a sudden collapse. The reasoning behind this remains unclear, with some historians speculating about everything from possible intrusion by outside forces to civil strife among the Myceneans themselves.

This left Greece in what has been termed a "dark age," followed by what has been called the Dorian invasion. This was when the Dorian sect of Greeks from the north came down and took over what little remained of the Mycenean settlements. This invasion, in turn, prompted some of the older settlers to cross over the Aegean Sea and create new settlements on the west coast of Anatolia (modern-day Turkey).

The Dorians, too, crossed the sea, except not in the direction of Anatolia but toward Crete, Rhodes, and Lycia. Over the next few centuries, not a whole lot is known. The Greek Dark Ages lasted until about 750 BCE before the brilliant light of the Hellenes began to shine forth once again.

Chapter 2 – Coming Out of the Dark Ages

"On a summer's night, I have sat on the balcony drinking Ouzo, watching the ghosts of Greek heroes sailing past, listening to the rustle of their sail cloths and the gentle lapping of their oars...and lain alongside Pythagoras watching him study the myriad of triangles in the constellations twinkling above us."

-Phil Simpkin

Around 750 BCE, Greece is believed to have come out of the Dark Ages, and once again, it embarked upon a marked advancement of civilization. This period, known as the Archaic Age, saw renewed commercial ties with the already thriving nations of the Middle East and Anatolia. These contacts allowed for the Greeks to adopt, among many other things, advanced metallurgy and an improved alphabet, the latter of which came by way of utilizing the Phoenician script to make improvements upon classical Greek writing.

As conditions began to improve on the Greek mainland, Greece experienced a kind of baby boom. Archaeological records show that there was a great increase in the population at this time, and this increase led to a renewed interest in the settlement of neighboring lands. As Greece became more crowded, those seeking more room to grow left for locales in the east, as well as settlements as far west as Sicily and Italy.

The term "Greek" itself came from the Italians, whom the Greeks came into contact with in Italy. Supposedly, it all stemmed from an incident in which Greek visitors were asked by Romans from where they had traveled, and the Greeks who had previously hailed from a settlement called Graia replied that it was from this town that they had come. The Romans, not realizing that these few Greeks were referring to one puny town rather than their entire homeland, thenceforth called all Greeks "Graeci," which in Latin simply meant "the people of Graia."

During this period, several prominent city-states began to dot the Greek landscape. The actual origin of the concept of the city-state is still a matter of argument for historians. Some have speculated that such a polis became desirable for the Greeks due to the nature of Greece's terrain, which featured flat plains nestled among majestic mountains. For them, it only made sense to form a centralized base in which people could forge a unified defense just in case someone happened to drop down from the highlands and attempted to ransack their settlements. And the fact that each of these city-states seems to revolve around already existing features of the environment seems to lend credence to this hypothesis.

These city-states were developed so that each city could stand as a strong, individual unit while also entering into commerce and communication with other neighboring city-states. And what was forged for the sake of common defense eventually became major commercial hubs and administrative centers.

On the other hand, the Myceneans, as great as they were, did not rely on the city-state structure but instead took top-down orders from their king. After Greece left the Dark Ages, the city-states came to prominence, and they were generally administered by the landed elite. This, of course, led to inevitable conflict between the upper class, landed gentry, and the poor, landless peasants who tilled their fields.

The Greek poet Hesiod made a note of this disparity in wealth in his piece, "Works and Days." Here, Hesiod illustrates just how hard life is for the toiling peasants and explains the growing animosity toward the landed elites. However, the major shift occurred when the city-states began to send emissaries across the seas and ushered in maritime riches that did not depend upon how much land one controlled.

By the 7th century, all of these factors led to tremendous societal upheaval in which the city-states came to be controlled by the so-called "tyrants." Although Greek in origin, the term is now quite familiar to English speakers, and no one in the English-speaking world would have any trouble at all understanding what a tyrant is. And as one might imagine, these original Greek tyrants were the same kind of power-hungry bullies, attempting to lord over everyone else through whatever tyrannical means were at their disposal.

Tyrants were typically members of the landed elite who had come to enough prominence to control city-states by force. This tyrannical leadership was naturally resented by the Greek people, but tyrannical control was not always so easily done away with. One famed tyrant, a man named Cypselus, ruled the Greek city of Corinth, and he was followed by an equally tyrannically ruler: his son, Periander. The two ruled for around seventy years, from 655 BCE to 585 BCE.

The people certainly groaned under their tyranny, yet at the same time, Corinth developed into a wealthy port city under the leadership of these two tyrants. So as tyrannical as they may have been, much of the city's wealth was due to their decisive actions. Such things were certainly not rare to the Greeks, and they have been repeated in other parts of the world throughout history.

Besides an occasional bent toward tyrannical rule and the consolidation of resources, another development of the city-state was the use of local militias. This phenomenon came to prominence due to the inability of city-states to sustain large armies. The best that could be done was to have citizens of the city being able and ready to take up arms when needed rather than having a huge professional army, which would need food and shelter on a regular basis.

In an effort to keep the volunteers for the city-state's militias in good fighting form, athletic contests were developed. During times of relative peace, members of the city's militia would compete in games of physical endurance with each other. These feats of endurance were localized, and they were primarily between individual citizens of that particular city-state.

In order to survive, the city-state forged ties of patriotic duty among its members for mutual defense. These militiamen became known as hoplites, and the average city-state could boast anywhere from three thousand to ten thousand of these hoplites at any given time. Along with defending the city-states, the hoplites actually became an important safeguard against encroaching tyranny. The city-state in which the hoplites most crucially performed this role was Sparta. It is said that Sparta was essentially tyranny-proof due to the efforts of its "hoplite government."

Yes, in Sparta, the hoplite warriors were more than just a mutual defense force; they actually became a part of the government itself. Sparta, which was situated on the flat plains near the Eurotas River, was actually an assortment of four closely connected settlements. And each of these settlements was run under a so-called "Spartan constitution," which featured an actual hoplite assembly that would meet to discuss matters important to the community. The Spartans were highly successful in both military matters and in the governance of their own domain.

That domain soon began to expand as the Spartans conquered neighboring regions. But as Sparta expanded, the difficulty of fielding a militia in sufficient numbers became increasingly more pronounced. As successful as the Spartan city-state may have been, any hope that the Spartans would become empire builders was apparently doomed to failure.

Nearby Athens, in the meantime, was having some pretty serious problems of its own. In the mid-600s, a tyrant named Theagenes was lording over the nearby city-state of Megara. Around 640 BCE, Theagenes began to threaten Athens. He and his son-in-law are said to have plotted a takeover of the city and tried to push out the landed elites so that the two could lord over the Athenians themselves. The attempt failed, but it led to the infamous Draco of Athens, who forged his so-called "Draconian" measures that he believed were needed to keep Athena prosperous.

As you have no doubt noted, the commonly used term "draconian," which means something drastic and desperate, takes its meaning from this incident. It is rather ironic that a man put in place to safeguard Athens from tyrants would impose laws that would essentially be viewed as extreme and tyrannical.

At any rate, around 620 BCE, the Draconian laws were codified in Athens. The exact details of the laws are not entirely clear, but it seems that punishment by death for even the most minor of infractions was quite common. The harshness of the Draconian laws created a backlash by the time of Solon in 594 BCE. Solon was made an archon (chief administrator) in Athens around this time, and he soon legislated a brand-new set of laws that, unlike the Draconian ones, tried to create a social compact that was strong yet far fairer in its implementation.

The major issue of Solon's day was the fact that the peasant farmers were being made to supply one-sixth of all of their harvest to landowners. These Draconian measures were considered harsh and often resulted in the peasants becoming indebted and ultimately enslaved by the rich landowners for whom they toiled. Solon solved this problem by easing the debts of the peasants while weakening the monopoly of the landed elite. With the stranglehold of the affluent broken, Solon then proceeded to broker a new system of governance in which he forged the boule, an assembly of some four hundred representatives comprised of one hundred members of each of the four main districts in Athens.

The archonship role of chief administrator, however, became a disputed position among the Athenians. This role continued to be a contentious issue, and it ultimately culminated in a successful seizure of power by yet another tyrant—Pesistratos. Pesistratos established a military dictatorship that lasted from 546 BCE to 510 BCE, when his son and successor, Hippias, was kicked out of power, finally ending the regime.

Even though this was essentially a strong-armed dictatorship, Pesistratos's regime was successful, both commercially and domestically. Under this tyrant's willful commands, major construction works were undertaken, creating lasting monuments to the tyrant who ordered their undertaking. By the 400s, the situation had changed, and the oligarch Cleisthenes decided to enter into a partnership with the common man of the city or, as the Greeks called them, the demos.

Cleisthenes then established ten groups of people, which were grouped together by location, in an attempt to bypass already established dynastic roots. It was these humble beginnings of democratic reform that would lead to the first full-blown democracy the world had ever known, which first came to prominence in Athens.

Chapter 3 – Athens and the Classical Era

"Socrates gave a lifetime to the outpouring of his substance in the shape of the greatest benefits bestowed on all who cared to receive them. In other words, he made those who lived in his society better men and sent them on their way rejoicing."

-Xenophon

The Greek Dark Ages were clearly over when the enlightened democracy of Athens took root in the 5th century BCE. Although we refer to Athens as being the place where democracy was born, by today's standards, it most certainly wouldn't be the kind of democracy of which we would approve. For one thing, only men who were born from an Athenian mother and father were allowed to participate in this democracy. Still, considering the times in which basically all societies were patriarchal (meaning male-dominated), Athenian democracy was indeed a significant advancement in human governance.

All Athenian-born men of Athens had the democratic right to speak their mind before the council and could actively vote for legislation of which they approved. This was a direct democracy. Even though modern nations, such as the United States, often boast that they are democracies, they are most certainly not direct democracies such as Athens was. If you live in the United States, for example, just ask yourself when was the last time you marched down to Congress and voted for a piece of legislation. You didn't. This is because the US uses a representative form of government, in which representatives the people vote for on Election Day go off to the nation's capital to represent their constituents and vote on their behalf in favor of or against the proposed legislation.

Athens, however, sported a direct democracy in which the people directly participated. Imagine a bunch of men in the town square being asked, "Men of Athens! Do you want to go to war with Sparta? Yes, or no?" This would be followed by a cacophony of yeses and noes being shouted until it was determined what the majority of Athenians wanted to do. This is direct democracy, a form of government with no presidents, no senators, no congresspeople, or any other form of representation.

Such a tradition, of course, took citizen participation to a whole new level, as the average Athenian had to show up to vote on just about any decision made by their society. Even more taxing, they also were expected to engage in voluntary service as magistrates themselves. In addition, the Athenians voted on their military leaders, voting for a total of ten different military chiefs every single year. The generals, therefore, were the elected officials who wielded the most power.

The greatest flaw of Greek democracy is said to have been a lack of will for citizens to galvanize themselves to action during crisis situations. For instance, imagine if a war was looming on the horizon, and half of the citizenry either failed to show up to vote or was completely bewildered as to what kind of action to take. As beautiful as direct democracy might sound, it soon takes on the trappings of an unintelligent, bickering mob with no idea what should be done and who should do it.

And this indecision could be devastating. It would not be good to have a heated debate among citizens while enemy troops were on the verge of beating down the doors to the assembly hall. This sort of dilemma presented itself during the Ionian revolt. The Ionian revolt involved a group of Greeks known as the Ionians who had founded Greek colonial outposts on the west coast of Asia Minor. By the 5th century, these outposts had been swallowed up by the growing Persian Empire.

In 499 BCE, the Ionians staged a revolt against their Persian overlords while they pleaded with their Greek counterparts on the mainland for help. The Spartans, for their part, flat-out refused since, as far as they were concerned, the Persians posed too distant of a threat to have to move their troops so far away. The Spartans were far too fearful of what might happen to Sparta if they left it undefended to mobilize any of their troops abroad.

Athens and the city-state of Eretria were more helpful, however, and agreed to come to the Ionians' aid. Athens, as it turns out, had some ulterior motives in mind since its burgeoning population was dependent upon shipments of corn and other supplies from Anatolia. Furthermore, Athens already had a bone to pick with Persia since Persian aggression in 514 BCE, under King Darius I (also known as Darius the Great), had disrupted Greek coastal communities and overseas commerce.

At any rate, as the battle heated up between the Ionians and the Persians, things came to a head when the Ionians assaulted the Persian administrative outpost of Sardis. The settlement was largely burned to the ground by the Ionians, although the Persian troops and administrators managed to hole up in a citadel and survive the onslaught. The whole effort proved to be rather fruitless, however, because shortly after, the Persians rallied and sent reinforcements that were easily able to dispatch the Ionian rabble-rousers.

Any self-respecting Athenians present at this point decided to head back to the mainland. Nevertheless, the Ionians continued to struggle with the Persians until they were decisively put down in 494 BCE. In the aftermath, the Athenians were kicking themselves over the relatively weak response of their fellow Greeks for the Ionians. This feeling of inadequacy was only reinforced a few years later in 490 BCE when the Persians decided to strike out against the Greek mainland itself.

The Persians hit Eretria first; the Eritreans held out for almost a week before they were forced to submit. And during the course of this struggle, no other Greek city-state took decisive action to defend them. They remained befuddled and indecisive in their assembly halls, unsure of what to do. Without facing any serious resistance, the Persians were then able to make their way to the Bay of Marathon to threaten Athens itself. Athens, realizing that it would need some help in repulsing the Persians, naturally sent emissaries to nearby Sparta to request aid.

Ridiculously enough, the Spartans refused the request on the grounds that they were celebrating a religious holiday. It sounds almost like a joke, but it is the truth. The completely unsympathetic Spartans refused to lend a hand to their neighboring city-state simply by stating that they had better things to do. This left Athens virtually by itself, with only the meager support of an obscure nearby settlement called Plataea (also spelled as Plataiai) to fend off the might of Persia.

But unlike the callous Spartans and despite their smaller stature in the Greek world, the Plataeans were determined to make a vigorous effort in coming to the aid of Athens, which had been a loyal ally to Plataea in the past. According to Greek historian Herodotus, lest the Athenians lose their nerve, they were all led out of the city to meet the threat head on. This meant marching from the gates of Athens some twenty-five miles to Marathon.

This twenty-five-mile stretch between Athens and Marathon is significant for another reason, as the modern-day meaning of a marathon is derived from an event that took place there. During the Battle of Marathon, a Greek soldier by the name of Pheidippides ran those twenty-five miles from Marathon to Athens to deliver the message that Persian forces had been bested in battle. According to legend, this messenger was so out of breath that he only had one word to shout to the Athenians, "Niki! Niki!" which is Greek for "Victory!"

Modern readers will note the similarity between "Niki" and a certain brand of running shoes called "Nike." Yes, Nike footwear does indeed take its name from the Greek word for victory. But the soldier-turned-messenger Pheidippides did not have long to celebrate the feeling of being victorious. According to legend, he was so exhausted after his marathon run that he keeled over and died! At any rate, it is from the events of this account that the term "marathon" has become associated with "long-distance running."

During the Battle of Marathon, the Athenians set up shop right on the road to Athens. Here, it is said that some ten thousand hoplites stood their ground, each holding a sword and a javelin, prepared to fight to the death. These ten thousand men were ultimately outnumbered by three to one when a force of some thirty thousand Persian troops marched right into their encampment.

But even though the Athenians were outnumbered three to one, they fought ferociously, and they were able to deliver an incredible number of casualties upon their attackers, forcing them to flee. This victory was spoken of with great pride many years later, and around 447 BCE, when the Parthenon was created, it was built with the defeat of the Persians in mind.

Interestingly enough, the Spartans who had refused to fight on the day that this ultimate showdown occurred actually arrived on the scene the next day when their services were conveniently no longer needed. One can only imagine the contempt the ancient Athenians must have felt for this belated show of support. Nevertheless, the Spartans themselves were most certainly overawed by what the Athenians had done. And it was after the victory of Marathon that the Athenians took the lead over the rest of the Greek city-states.

Chapter 4 – United They Stand

"Anybody can become angry—that is easy. But to be angry with the right person and to the right degree and at the right time and for the right purpose, and in the right way—that is not within everybody's power and is not easy."

-Epicurus

After their advances were rolled back by the Athenians, the Persians bitterly plotted their revenge. It would be the Persian who took the helm after Darius—Xerxes—who would next lead an assault not just on Athens but also the Greek civilization as a whole. And this time, nothing would be given to chance. Every aspect of the campaign would be meticulously planned.

The Persian warriors were heavily armed and well provisioned. Even so, it was made sure that plenty of "supply dumps" would be buried under the ground all along the way to Athens. Several naval craft, in the meantime, were massing along the Bosporus in Anatolia, preparing for an invasion. However, the Greek city-states of the mainland initially seemed to take little notice amidst their squabbling with one another.

But as the threat continued to grow, clearer heads finally prevailed. And in 481 BCE, an assembly of Greek city-states managed to gather together at Corinth to discuss a joint strategy against the Persians. This alliance would become known as the Hellenic League. The dominant power player of this league was Sparta, which, despite its previous dithering, carried the most obvious military might. But even once the league was brought together, there was still quite a bit of bickering as to what the best path forward would be.

The Spartans wished to stand their ground in Corinth, but such a move would leave the entire center of the Greek mainland defenseless. Athens, on the other hand, wished to pursue the Persians on the northern front of Greece. After many arguments were made, it was finally determined that a unified army would be sent to the Vale of Tempe in the northern reaches of Thessaly.

Upon reaching Thessaly, however, it was understood that the Persian forces could easily outflank the Greeks. The strategy then shifted again, and it was decided it would be better to shut off access to the south of the country instead. This led to some seven thousand Spartan troops being placed at Thermopylae. Led by the famed King Leonidas of Sparta, the Spartan forces held off a much larger Persian army for about two days. However, the Persians were tipped off about a secret path, which enabled them to go around the amassed Spartans. Leonidas, realizing that he and his men were doomed, allowed those who wished to flee to leave, but he remained with some one thousand loyal troops to fight the Persians to the death.

Those Spartans were destroyed, all of northern Greece was in peril, and, once again, the Athenians were forced to face the Persians alone. The average Athenian citizens were evacuated to higher ground. The Persians showed up in Athens only to find a meager residual force who fought to defend the Acropolis. This group was easily put down, and the city was looted.

However, the Greeks weren't completely beat yet. The Greek navy managed to lure the Persian forces into waging war in the waters between Greece and the Isle of Salamis, and the Persian ships became trapped, allowing the Greek naval forces to pick the Persians off one by one.

This was a major setback to the Persians, but the war was far from over. Winter was setting in, and the Persians decided to hold the ground they had in Greece and wait until spring to reengage the remaining resistance. The final showdown occurred in Plataea, where resurgent Greek forces were able to drive the Persians off the mainland completely. It was only through the unification of the remnants of Greek power that the Persians were finally defeated.

With all the Greek factions united and with the mighty Spartans leading the pack, they marched right up the Isthmus of Corinth to meet the Persians on land. It was near the city of Attica that this climactic fight erupted. The Persians were able to charge the Greek formations on horseback, and Persian arrows inflicted terrible losses, but in the end, the Greeks were able to stand up to the Persian threat and halt their advance. Not only that, in the immediate aftermath, the Greeks were able to regain the lost Ionian colonies in Anatolia.

This sequence of events would prove to be a powerful lesson to the early Greek democracies of just how important unity was for survival, and it would lead the way toward uniting the city-states into one single polity. It was for this reason, after all, that the powerful Hellenic League was formed in the first place. It was established in order to create a stronger compact between all of the Greek city-states in common defense against outside aggression. And predictably enough, it was Athens that would take the lead in this charter.

Persia would again threaten the Greek lands in 466 BCE when a fleet was sent to skirmish with Greek troops in the Aegean Sea near the coast of Anatolia. Known as the Battle of the Eurymedon River, here, once again, the Persians were defeated. Thanks to the cooperation of the Hellenic League, the Persians had been checked on both the land and the sea. As a result of this triumph, the Persians would not be able to menace the Greeks again for several more decades.

The fact that the Greeks were able to stop what was then the world's greatest empire in its tracks was an impressive feat, and the glory of the Greeks' triumph was not lost on them. They would long celebrate the victories of Marathon and Salamis, instilling themselves with an unbridled sense of national pride. Also, the fact that the league was maintained even after the Persian threat was eliminated demonstrates that the strength of solidarity was deemed to be crucial for Greek survival.

But even though the Greeks managed to stand toe to toe with the Persian Empire, as soon as their unity dissolved, they would be at each other's throats. With the defeat of the Persians, the Greeks had shown that they could stand strong when united together. But as the years progressed, cracks in their social compact would emerge, and it would prove increasingly difficult for them to hold it together. Early on, one of the first points of friction occurred when some members of the union attempted to break away due to what was perceived as an overreach by Athens.

The primary reason that Athens was able to maintain dominance was due to the city-state's powerful navy. If anyone fell out of line, it would not take much for Athens to scramble a fleet together to poke and prod the rebels back into conformity. And in some cases, members were even forced into the compact against their will. This happened with Karystos and the island of Skyros, which were both forcibly coerced into the union. Even more infamous was the subjugation of the Cycladic island of Melos, which was forced into Athens's orbit around the year 416 BCE. This coercion resulted in the massacre of countless inhabitants of the island and others being outright enslaved. Most historians would agree that this was a clear overreach of the Athenians, who otherwise have often been painted as the idyllic forgers of democracy. Yes, they may have created some aspects of the democratic ideal, but the actions of this democracy were often less than ideal for those on the periphery.

Relations with Sparta had greatly deteriorated by this time, giving rise to the Peloponnesian War, which lasted from 431 BCE to 404 BCE. The war was called as such because, during this great rift in Greek relations, Sparta had rallied the city-states of the Peloponnesian League in the Peloponnesian region of Greece. The Spartans and the Peloponnesians had decided to stand up to what they perceived as the "imperialism" of Athens.

The Spartans also wanted to make sure that they maintained control of the mainland and stayed strong in case of revolts from within their sphere of influence. And they could only stay strong if Athens was kept in check. Hostilities actually erupted when Corinth fought back against Athenian pressure. In 432 BCE, Corinth began to have trouble with the nearby Greek settlement of Corfu (also known as Kerkyra). After hostilities between these two settlements commenced, Corfu asked Athens for help. Athens agreed, but it angered Sparta in doing so since the Spartans were allied to Corinth.

During the war, both sides had their own advantages. Athens's major advantage was its naval power, whereas Sparta's advantage was the size of its hoplite infantry forces on land. In 425 BCE, Athens managed to take 120 Spartan troops as prisoners of war. This might not seem like much, but since Spartans had pledged to fight to their deaths, the fact that so many were captured managed to erode the reputation of Spartan prowess in battle.

This was then followed by a group of Athenian naval craft heading around the western shores of the Peloponnese. The Spartans feared that this would be used as a launching pad to attack Sparta and took decisive action. They sent a group of Spartans to face the threat and attempted to lay siege to the Athenians stationed on the Peloponnese. However, the Athenians simply sent another fleet of ships to intercept them, and pretty soon, the Spartans themselves were being overwhelmed by the Athenians.

Sparta continued to struggle in the larger war, and in 418 BCE, the Spartans struck a victory of their own by knocking Athens's ally Argos out of the war. The Spartans then continued to rack up gains against Athens, and in 412 BCE, they even managed to forge an alliance with the old Greek foe of Persia through the local Greek satrap (a local ruler) Tissaphernes, which enabled Persian Emperor Darius II to sweep down into western Anatolia to reclaim the Greek cities in Ionia. Darius II then sent his own son Cyrus to the region to oversee Persian efforts in person.

The next major turning point in this war occurred in 405 BCE when the Athenian navy was destroyed. Bereft of a navy, food and other goods soon ceased to arrive in Athens's ports. The Spartans were now well positioned to starve their enemies into submission. And so, with pressure building on all sides, the city of Athens was finally forced to surrender in 404 BCE.

But even though Athens was defeated, the power politics of the Greek city-states managed to save the city from total annihilation. The supposed allies of Sparta, namely Thebes and Corinth, still wanted Athens around as a check against the strength of Sparta itself. They did not mind weakening Athens and stripping the city-state's extraterritorial lands from it, but they wanted the city itself to remain mostly intact as a bulwark against total domination by Sparta.

In the end, like an unruly child called to task, Athens was forced to become a partner with Sparta and the other Greek city-states once again. Athens had seemingly grown too powerful for its own good, only for it to be knocked back in line with its fellow city-states. This could have been a chance for a renewed sense of unity, but it would not be long before an outside power would rise up to take advantage of the lingering instability.

Chapter 5 – The Dangers of Democracy

"For myself, I think that those who cultivate wisdom and believe themselves able to instruct their fellow-citizens as to their interests are least likely to become partisans of violence. They are too well aware that to violence attach enmities and dangers, whereas results as good may be obtained by persuasion safely and amicably."

-Xenophon

In the aftermath of Athens's defeat by Sparta, the democratic institutions that had flourished in the city-state were dismantled. In its place rose what can only be termed an oligarchy, which was controlled by just a few of the landed elites. This ushered in a period that would become known as the time of the Thirty Tyrants. These brutish enforcers were backed up by the power of a small Spartan encampment stationed right in the middle of Athens's Acropolis.

Completely devolving from a democracy to a petty oligarchy, many of Athens's brightest, pro-democracy minds began to form a sort of exiled intelligentsia. These renegades eventually found a home in Attica, where they were protected by Thebans who were unhappy with the heavy-handedness of the Spartans. They also managed to flourish in the nearby town of Piraeus, where they gained support from the locals. When it became widely known that these pockets of resistance were developing, the tyrants of Athens and their handlers from Sparta began to mobilize themselves to purge the democrats from their midst.

They were initially successful, but due to pushback against the subsequent harshness and austerity, a middle-of-the-road approach was developed, in which more moderate forms of democracy were allowed to take root once again in the city of Athens. If anyone was viewed to have stepped outside the bounds of this newfound moderation, however, they were quickly punished.

Shortly after this restoration, one of the greatest of Greek tragedies is said to have transpired. For it was around 399 BCE that the Greek philosopher Socrates suffered persecution and was ultimately executed by Greek authorities.

Socrates himself is not known to have written anything down, and what we know of this great teacher actually comes down to us from one of his later protégés—Plato. Socrates taught his pupils to think freely, but the Athenian authorities soon became alarmed and felt that he was teaching them to think just a little bit too freely. And after some of his teachings were uncovered by the powers that be, he was actually charged with the so-called crime of "corrupting the youth," as well as general "impiety."

The impiety charge was apparently on the grounds that he was accused of worshiping false deities while failing to adhere to the proper state religion. Socrates did not deny these charges since he was indeed one to openly criticize the anthropomorphic nature of Greek's old belief system. At any rate, these alleged "crimes" landed Socrates in the courtroom. Socrates didn't have an attorney; he defended himself.

During the course of the trial, he clearly expressed his beliefs and the reasons behind his actions. His efforts would become known as a Socratic apology, and his methods, as described by

Plato, would later be known as the Socratic method. This is a method of debate that employs a question-and-answer, conversational format in order to prove a point and provide critical analysis of a subject.

Despite all of his skills of reason, Socrates was ultimately unable to turn the tide against him. Socrates was found guilty, and he was sentenced to death. He was forced to drink a cup of poisonous hemlock. It is said that one of the constant threads of Socrates's teachings is to embrace death without any fear or hesitation. Socrates apparently wanted to practice what he had been teaching and gladly took the cup he was given without any sign of fear or trepidation. And when others around him began to cry, he was quick to tell them to wipe away their tears. Socrates assured them that death was not a big deal but rather just a normal transition that we all must undergo at some point in our life.

It was Socrates's noble death that made him a martyred icon in the eyes of his students and the subsequent followers of his philosophy. The most important thing that Socrates's life and teaching exposed about democratic societies is the realization that just because the majority of the people in a democracy decide to do something, it does not mean their decision is a good one.

Socrates was killed by the unanimous consensus of a mob mentality. Yes, a jury of his peers democratically decided to kill him, but just because the majority of those operating the levers of Athens's democracy decided to end his life, it does not mean that this decision was an ethical one. Interestingly enough, the Founding Fathers of America were also very much afraid of developing a democracy with a mob mentality, and they looked toward the lesson of Socrates as a great warning against the dangers of such things. America's Founding Fathers knew full well that all manner of horrible things could occur when a huge mob of people get caught up in the moment and decide to do something. James Madison, for one, had actively read up on the example of the direct democracy of

Athens and clearly saw how unbridled, dangerous passions of a momentary majority could wreak untold havoc on society. After all, in a moment of passion, it takes a while for the cooler heads to prevail.

Yet, if decisions were made by six hundred citizens screaming in an assembly immediately after a call to action is made, the cooler heads would never get the chance to consider the possibilities. The Founding Fathers knew that this could lead to disastrous and completely wrong decisions on the part of the democratic masses. What if, for example, in ancient Greece, the Acropolis mysteriously burned down one night, with a rumor emerging that Corinth was behind it? Before the facts are even known, you could have the assembly packed with an entire mob of citizens demanding action being taken against Corinth. In a direct democracy like Athens, this could lead to an authentically democratic decision being made to wage war against Corinth. Yet, suppose that right after much bloodshed against the Corinthians had ensued, the Athenians learned that Corinth actually had nothing to do with the fire at the Acropolis and the whole thing was all just a big accident.

Well, this is exactly what the Founding Fathers' fears were when they shuddered at the notion of a "mobocracy" run amuck. Or as James Madison stated in the *Federalist Papers* at America's founding, "In all very numerous assemblies, of whatever characters composed, passion never fails to wrest the scepter from reason." He then even went on to note, "Had every Athenian citizen been a Socrates, every Athenian assembly would still have been a mob."

In other words, even if assembled citizens were of the best character, they could—as the above example demonstrates—become very easily confused and inflamed in the passion of the moment, leading to bad decisions being made. It was for this reason that the Founding Fathers eschewed direct democracy for a representative republic in which democratically elected representatives are (hopefully) enlightened enough to understand what is in the best interest of their constituents. And if they fail to vote for legislation that benefits their constituents, they can be democratically voted out in favor of other representatives who promise to do so.

At any rate, immediately after the death of Socrates, the mob rule of Athens was pushed aside when the Spartans decided to clamp down and take on greater control. As one might expect, the other Greek city-states soon grew resentful of this overreach by Sparta, just as they did when it was Athens lording over them. And by 394 BCE, Thebes and Corinth were teaming up with Athens to wage against Sparta in what became known as the Corinthian War.

The war ended up being a big, bloody stalemate, with neither side gaining any real advantage. But perhaps the oddest part of the whole thing was the fact that the old enemies of the Greeks, the Persians, were the ones who actually mediated a truce between them in 387 BCE. This cessation of fighting became known as the King's Peace, so named after the Persian king at the time, Artaxerxes II.

The King's Peace, however, would not be the final say in who would dominate the Greek world. For shortly thereafter, Athens joined a new alliance with other city-states and rose up to challenge its antagonists. Called the Second Athenian League, this union consisted of Athens along with a smattering of city-states of the Ionian and Aegean Seas. This alliance was markedly different from previous ones since Athens, apparently learning lessons from its past, made a real effort to not lord over its allies.

But although this was indeed more considerate for its partners, it also created a vacuum of leadership, and the Second Athenian League quickly proved to be too indecisive to make any real difference in the power politics of the Mediterranean world. The next attempt at peacemaking occurred in 371 BCE when Athens and Sparta, along with Persia, brought about plans for a general peace.

Sparta's rival Thebes initially indicated that it would sign off on the agreement, but it was only willing to do so if it was allowed to represent the Boeotian cities. Boeotia is a region of central Greece of which Thebes is a part. So essentially, the Thebans wanted to be recognized as the main player from their district.

The Spartans, however, did not want Thebes to take a leading role among the Boeotian cities and rejected the offer outright. Instead, the king of Sparta, Cleombrotos, decided to march directly on the region to subjugate it. The Thebans and Spartans then faced off against each other on the plain of Leuctra. The Thebans were able to defeat the Spartans, and King Cleombrotos was killed during the course of the conflict. This marked the end of Spartan dominance in the region.

Interestingly enough, however, in a virtual replay of what had happened to Athens many years before, the significantly weakened Sparta ended up aligning itself with its old nemesis of Athens so that the two could present a united front against the suddenly resurgent power of Thebes. But it wasn't Thebes that Athens had to worry about but rather a surprise incursion from neighboring Macedonia when a man named Alexander wished to make himself great.

Chapter 6 – The Rise of Macedonia

"You see—Oh Greeks! The Enemy already acknowledge the country to be ours; for when they made peace with us, they stipulated that we should not burn the country belonging to the king, and now they set fire to it themselves, as if they looked upon it no longer as their own."

-Xenophon

Even while the Greek city-states were weakening each other with all of their intermittent skirmishes, Macedonia to the north of Greece proper was steadily increasing its might. Unlike the Greeks, the Macedonians did not reside in city-states and loose confederations but rather in an autocratic kingdom with centralized authority over the entire nation state. Although Macedonia has at times been considered a Greek-influenced region, actual Greeks did not consider the Macedonians a part of their heritage.

Since the Macedonians did not have a good handle on the Greek language and did not have a form of governance with which the Greeks were familiar, such as a democracy or an oligarchy, the Greeks considered the Macedonians as hopeless outsiders. So, it is a little ironic that it was these "outsiders" who would come to spread the Greek language and culture all over the known world.

Nevertheless, the Greeks had long looked down on Macedonians as being their backward, uncivilized, and unenlightened neighbors. And for much of its early history, Macedonia was also known to be militarily inferior to its Greek neighbors. But by the 300s, all this was steadily changing. The Macedonian monarchy was growing in strength, and so, too, were its armies. The first truly promising and strong Macedonian leader came in the form of King Philip II in 357 BCE.

Philip would build Macedonia's military up to be the most formidable in the region. Later Greek historians would attribute this accomplishment to the force of Philip's own personality. It seems that Philip was able to unite Macedonia even while the Greek city-states remained divided. He was then able to use this united front to take full advantage of his hopelessly divided neighbors.

It wasn't always smooth sailing for King Philip, however, and he had to work to gain the dominance that he eventually achieved. At the beginning of his reign, he had inherited a divisive and fractured kingdom. But through Philip's skill as a politician, he was able to bring the factions of his kingdom together. He also wasn't above bribing or even assassinating those with whom he didn't see eye to eye. Whatever it took, Philip muscled and manipulated his way to unquestioned authority.

And once he was at the top, he made sure that Macedonia's troops were well trained and ready to fight. He built up his army primarily on the lower classes, with whom he had developed a cult of personality in which he was at the center. Along with military might, Philip also recognized the importance of culture, in particular, Greek culture. He knew that the Greeks had forged a very unique and powerful form of civilization, and he wished to emulate it within his own kingdom.

As such, he established a brand-new Hellenized capital in Macedonia, which he called Pella. He also recruited some Greek advisors into his own inner circle. The Greek city-states, in the meantime, began to take notice of Macedonia's ambition. Greek politician Demosthenes was particularly astute as to what Philip was up to, and he openly warned people about it in several lectures called the *Philippics*.

Despite this early warning from the likes of Demosthenes, the tidings of impending doom were mostly ignored. In the meantime, Macedonian King Philip was on the march, waging war and taking territory by force. And soon, he had incorporated several of Greece's northernmost city-states into his empire. He then surprised everyone by annexing territory to his east, which gave him direct control of Mount Pangaeus, which had valuable silver and gold mines.

Philip now had not only a sound army but also sound finances with which to consolidate his base even further. With his fortunes even further secured, he managed to pressure Thessaly into entering a partnership with him and then pushed his influence onto several other Greek city-states. Throughout all of this, Thebes had become considerably weaker after several years of battling its neighboring city-state of Phocis, a struggle that often revolved around who had access to the sanctuary of Delphi, which was located in Phocis.

Even though Phocis was smaller than Thebes, the fact that they oversaw the sanctuary of Delphi, where many Greek pilgrims visited and left offerings of gold, silver, and the like, meant they had tremendous resources at their disposal to hire outside fighters to engage their enemies. Thus, Phocis was able to fight off the more powerful Thebes for several years. It was only in 346 that Philip decided to put his thumb on the scale in this seemingly never-ending conflict between the two city-states and coerced them both into coming to terms.

It was only after this direct and obvious foreign interference from Macedonia that Athens became truly alarmed and entered into an alliance with Thebes. These developments ultimately led to a showdown between Philip and these two Greek allies when the Macedonian king sent his army to Athens in 338 BCE. The forces of Athens and Thebes were ill-prepared to stand up to what amounted to the most well-trained military force in the region. Philip's troops moved in machine-like precision, moving forward in a solid formation with their long pikes with which they steadily tore through their enemies.

In addition to the pike-wielding infantry, the Macedonians also employed a cavalry that could quickly strike out at the enemy before pulling back. At the onset of the battle, the Greeks actually had the numerical advantage, fielding a force of about thirty-eight thousand troops compared to the Macedonians' thirty-two thousand, but the ferocious pikemen of Philip very rapidly bridged that gap. The cavalry, which was led by Philip's soon-to-be-famous son Alexander, was also quite good at decimating the Greek defenders.

At one point during the battle, the Theban forces had stretched themselves too thin, and Alexander was able to lead the cavalry full-force into the vulnerable section of the Theban line, smashing right through their ranks. This cut the army in half and allowed Alexander and his men to completely decimate the cornered Thebans. The entire Greek defense fell apart shortly after that, and soon, the Macedonians were in complete control of the situation.

But unlike the worst fears of Demosthenes, who predicted the complete destruction of the Greek city-states if Philip took over, Philip showed a surprising amount of benevolence to those he had just vanquished. No petty retributions were conducted; instead, the Greek city-states were simply asked to become partners with Macedonia. In order to show their respect for the Athenians, Philip even went as far as to have Alexander personally deliver the ashes of those Athenians who had perished in the conflict.

The Greeks were almost relieved at the results of their defeat, and only Sparta would remain hesitant in accepting the dominance of Macedonia. To make things official, one year after his successful military campaign, Philip brought the Greek leaders together in Corinth and had them swear their undying support to Macedonia in what would become known as the League of Corinth, also sometimes known simply as the Hellenic League.

This Hellenic League would become the unified force that would spread Macedonian-led conquests far and wide. For all of the freedoms of democracy, it was the top-down nature of Macedonia's centralized government, headed by a Macedonian king, that enabled the consistency necessary for true empire-building. First Philip and then his son Alexander would come to steadily dominate much of the known world.

But not everyone in the Greek-speaking world was so thrilled about being a part of this dynamic imperialist machine. The Macedonians were viewed as outsiders, and the idea that the independent city-states would have to follow the mandates of this outside force was, in their eyes, the worst kind of tyranny. Even worse than the thirty tyrants was the tyranny of this foreign influence from Macedonia.

Philip himself was well aware of this lack of trust, and the crafty and cunning politician in him wanted to find a way to bring his Greek subjects into a more authentic allegiance. An Athenian political leader by the name of Isocrates brought Philip the key he was looking for to unify the masses. Isocrates urged Philip to bring the Greek city-states together on a campaign to take on the old enemy of the Greeks—the Persians. Having a common enemy certainly does tend to bring folks together, and Philip readily agreed with this strategy.

And so it was at the dawning of the League of Corinth that Philip made clear his plans of sending the whole Greek-speaking world once again on a crash course with the Persian civilization. A year after this pronouncement, Philip sent his general Parmenion to make his way to Anatolia so that the first stepping stone toward an all-out invasion could be made.

All of the machinery for this great conquest was already in place, but the man behind the wheel would soon be taken from the helm. Philip, as powerful as he was, had become surrounded by much intrigue in his personal court. Philip had a total of six women whom he called his wife, but only one of these brides was considered his queen—Alexander's mother, Olympias.

Queen Olympias was of royal stock; she had formerly been a princess of Epirus or what today would be considered the country of Albania before she married King Philip. Initially, Alexander was Philip's only potential successor, and he had been groomed as such. Alexander had what in those days amounted to the finest in education, being personally tutored by the great Greek scholar Aristotle. But in 336 BCE, Philip took yet another woman to be his bride, which caused a rift between him and both Alexander and Olympias.

Philip ultimately divorced Olympias and had her sent back to her homeland of Epirus, which was a part of the ancient Greek world that today constitutes part of Albania. But even though King Philip had divorced his wife, she was still the mother of the heir to the throne and, therefore, held some considerable clout. However, there were some decidedly nasty rumors floating about that threatened to take even her claim as the mother of the heir apparent away from her.

At the heart of the drama seems to be insinuations that Olympia had been unfaithful to Philip, and there even gossip that Alexander might be illegitimate. Although these rumors seem to be unfounded and perhaps were purposefully started by Philip himself, there was some fear that Alexander could be demoted. Alexander and his mother knew that any potential offspring from his father's new union could somehow disrupt Alexander's own destiny.

However, most historians dismiss this since Alexander was the oldest son, and he was already well on his way to becoming Philip's heir. Nevertheless, there was tension in regard to Philip's new wife and what might result from their pairing. Despite the drama, Philip and Alexander managed to reconcile for a time, and Alexander even attended his father's wedding. But things quickly got out of hand when one of Philip's generals allegedly gave a toast to Philip and his new wife, wishing their union to produce a "legitimate" heir for Macedonia.

If this event really did occur (historians are still unsure if it did or not), it would have been an obvious snub to Alexander and his right to succeed his father. And Alexander wasn't going to take such an insult sitting down. According to tradition, he jumped right up onto his feet. Staring down the general who dared to say such hurtful words, he took the cup of wine he was holding and hurled it into the general's face. Philip was apparently ready to side with his general over his own son and immediately stood up with his sword drawn.

But Philip only managed to take a few steps toward Alexander before he stumbled, tripped, and fell to the ground. Philip had apparently drunk way too much for his own good and lost his footing. Some might speculate that it is possible that Philip only pretended to be drunk as a means of avoiding a full-blown confrontation with his son. As crude as such a ruse was, it would have saved Philip some face. No one present could say that he did not answer his son's challenge, yet at the same time, he could avoid actually hurting his son by blaming his inaction on being drunk.

At any rate, after his dad's stumble, Alexander angrily ridiculed his father, declaring, "Look, everyone! The man who wants to cross Europe to Asia can't even make it from one couch to the next!" After this dramatic event, Alexander went to live in Epirus, where his exiled mother Olympias was staying at the time. While he was away, Philip's new wife gave birth to a baby.

However, this child was no threat to Alexander since she was a female, and as was the case with just about all monastic dynasties of the day, the male typically inherited the throne. New tidings then came to Alexander shortly thereafter that his father was planning to marry Alexander's sister, who was also a child of Queen Olympia, to an uncle of his in Epicurus.

Back in those days, it wasn't at all uncommon for a niece to marry an uncle, a nephew to marry an aunt, or cousins to marry each other. Today, such things would be viewed as bizarre, but back then, it was considered acceptable, especially within royal families that were attempting to solidify dynastic bonds. And this arranged marriage to a relative in Epicurus was apparently Philip's attempt to build some new bridges over the previous ones he had burned.

As was customary, Philip once again staged an elaborate wedding banquet, and of course, Alexander was invited. Alexander, seeking to mend fences, obliged his father and attended. But there would be even more drama afoot, this time not involving Alexander at all but rather a spurned courtesan by the name of Pausanias. The exact details of what led to this assassin's grievance against Philip are a bit murky, but it seems that a deep personal animosity had developed.

At the king's court, Pausanias is said to have been a personal favorite of King Philip, and according to some accounts, the two were even said to be lovers. Philip, however, had a roving eye and started seeking the favors of another male paramour. Pausanias was upset about all of this, and he began a vicious gossip campaign against the new lover, slandering him in all kinds of ways. But what apparently hurt the man the most was the slanderous remarks in which he was accused of being a coward.

In the rough-and-tumble world of ancient Macedonia, bravery meant everything. And to prove his bravery, the ridiculed young man went to the front lines of the Macedonian army. He ended up being killed in battle as a result. Both Philip and his top general, Attalus, were upset with what had transpired.

Attalus, for his part, was beside himself with rage that Pausanias would commit what he viewed as being an entirely dastardly and cowardly act. The man who died as a result of Pausanias's machinations also happened to be a friend of his. So, it was with this frame of mind that Attalus decided to take justice (albeit his warped sense of it) into his own hands and punish Pausanias.

And Attalus would do so with the most insidious of intrigue by initially befriending Pausanias. He actually invited Pausanias over to a get-together with some of his other friends. They plied Pausanias with alcohol until he was incapacitated. And when Pausanias was too drunk to resist, his utter humiliation began. The men took off Pausanias's clothes and proceeded to gang-rape him.

As soon as he had recovered enough to do so, Pausanias sought out King Philip in order to punish Attalus and his other attackers. Philp is said to have genuinely felt sorry for his former friend, but since he needed his trusted general on the front lines, he opted not to pursue any charges. It is said that this humiliation burned in Pausanias's mind so much that he decided to take Philip's life.

Of course, all of this is ultimately speculation since Pausanias was struck down and killed shortly after he committed the act. Pausanias would not live long enough to give his own personal account for his actions. After stabbing Philip right through the heart, Pausanias attempted to make a break for it. There was nowhere for the killer to run, however, and he was quite easily intercepted. And rather than arresting him and questioning him as to his motives, he was simply killed right there on the spot.

For some, things appear to have happened a little too conveniently. Could it be that there was a larger plot afoot that involved Queen Olympias? What if she had hired Pausanias to kill the king? If she had, it is possible that she covered her tracks by ordering those close to her to immediately kill the assassin after he carried out the hit. Dead men don't talk after all. This is all just conjecture, of course, and much about what really happened to

King Philip remains a mystery. The sudden rise of Philip's son Alexander to greatness, however, is not.

Chapter 7 – Enter Alexander the Great

"Those who intend on becoming great should love neither themselves nor their own things, but only what is just, whether it happens to be done by themselves or others."

-Plato

After Philip II's sudden demise in 336 BCE, his son Alexander was named king of Macedon at just twenty years of age. Alexander wasted no time in getting his house in order. Knowing that loyalty was everything, he made sure to reshuffle the deck of courtesans to those who were most sympathetic to him. Alexander then looked abroad, where whispers of rebellion began to surface among the recently conquered Greek city-states, which wished to test the will of the young new ruler.

Alexander knew all too well that he had to present a strong face to these subject nations if he was going to be able to keep the Hellenic League together. The first to test the new king was Thessaly, which had begun its rebellion by blocking off certain roadways in and out of the region. It was not the worst offense that the Thessalonians could have engaged in, but Alexander knew that if he didn't come down on them—and come down hard—this trespass would only lead to more.

Thus, Alexander was determined to march right over to Thessaly to knock some heads. And the way he did so was rather ingenious. For even though the Thessalonians had blocked the roads into the region, Alexander simply had his engineers build a new road through the rear of the mountain passes. The Thessalonians, who were actively guarding the other side of the mountains, were horrified to find Alexander and his army suddenly drop on top of them. The battle quickly turned into a rout, and the desperate Thessalonians were forced to quickly come to terms.

With the Thessalonians groveling at his feet, Alexander then marched south to Thebes. Ever since Philip's death, the Thebans had been restless and were considering an open rebellion just like the Thessalonians. All it took to change their minds was the sight of Alexander at the head of his massive army, galloping up to the outskirts of their city. Without any struggle at all, the Thebans agreed to recognize Alexander's authority.

After subduing Thebes, Alexander went over to Thermopylae and found them to be already compliant. And every region he visited seemed equally compliant until, finally, Alexander reached Corinth, and in full sight of the representatives of the League of Corinth, he was proclaimed as the "leader for life."

Shortly after this proclamation, a rather conspicuous incident is said to have occurred. While Alexander was camped in Corinth, a man wandered into the city, claiming to have been attacked by Persian troops who were harassing the neighboring city of Ephesus. It would later be learned that the man was actually someone Alexander had hired to pretend to be a war-torn refugee in order to stoke the flames of Greek resentment against the Persians. But it worked. The League of Corinth was indignant that the Persians would attack one of their own. Fully confident in the might of

Macedonia, the city-states agreed to throw in their lot in a renewed war against Persia.

Early on, fractures in this alliance would emerge. And predictably—if not outrageously—enough, it was the Thebans who once again began to rebel against Alexander. It is a bit hard to fathom how Thebes could consider rebelling against Alexander so soon after a previous rebellion had been put down, but it seems that the Greek politician Demosthenes might have had something to do with it. Demosthenes was a popular speaker and was making his rounds in Athens. He was known to stir folks to action just by the sound of his voice. This time, however, he was apparently spreading outright falsehoods, for he started to circulate the claim that Alexander had perished on the front lines.

When this bit of fake news reached Thebes, the Thebans got excited and decided to rebel once again. It must have come as quite a shock when the Macedonian monarch showed up on the outskirts of their city alive and well. This time, there would be no fighting but rather outright annihilation. Alexander burned the city to the ground. The rest of the Greek city-states took the lesson of Thebes to heart, and attempts at rebellion soon ceased.

With everyone else falling in behind him, Alexander could finally focus on what he really wanted—a Pan-Hellenic conquest of the East. Alexander and his armies reached Anatolia around 337 BCE, and with an army of some forty thousand troops—one-fourth of which were likely Greek—the march toward the Persian Empire commenced. Initially, Alexander's forces were greeted as liberators since they were primarily encountering the Greek settlements on the Anatolian coast.

The first encounter with Persian forces occurred farther east at Granikos River, just outside of the outskirts of a city called Priapus. Alexander's forces were outnumbered by the Persians, but he urged his comrades on. Upon making contact with the enemy, a pitched battle ensued in which both sides fought with ferocious desperation.

Alexander himself quickly became a target due to his brightly shining armor. It seems that he was easily recognized as the leader of the group, and due to the gleam of his regalia, Persian arrows were quick to find their mark.

At one point, even a Persian swordsman was able to get close enough to the Macedonian to strike the back of his helmeted head. The sword cut right through Alexander's helmet and went through skin and bone. It was just a flesh wound, but it was a gruesome one at that. Fortunately for Alexander, this was the closest the Persians would get to him. And it was not for lack of trying.

Alexander's ostentatious armor made him stand out, so the Persians began zeroing in on him. They became so obsessed about it, in fact, that they opened themselves up to being butchered by making blind charges toward Alexander's heavily guarded position. Macedonian troops cut down Persian after Persian as they forgot all else and threw themselves headlong at Alexander. They must have thought that by taking out the leader, the battle would end, but after they were unable to do so, all they had to show for their efforts was the wasted lives of countless Persian troops. Soon, the Persians death toll was too high for them to continue their efforts, and they decided to make a run for it.

After this first victory against the Persians, Alexander famously ordered his men to gather up about three hundred suits of armor from slain or captured Persians, and he had it sent off to Athens. He proclaimed that these trophies were dedicated to Athena as some kind of good luck charms to bring him further victories. Alexander then marched on to Ephesus, the very place from which news of a false flag attack had originated. The Ephesians did not welcome Alexander with open arms; on the contrary, the town, despite its heavy Greek population, initially attempted to put up a resistance. It was a fleeting one, however, and in rather short order, Alexander's mighty army convinced them otherwise.

Since this is a book on Greek history and not a book on the deeds of the Macedonian Alexander the Great, delving too much into his exploits can be distracting. So as not to get too off track, Alexander's conquests can be summarized as follows. After bringing Anatolia to heel, Alexander headed south to Syria, which was also a part of Persian Emperor Darius III's domain. It was there, in Syria, that Darius himself led his army to a colossal confrontation with Alexander and his men.

The two forces collided near the town of Issos (also spelled as Issus). The wide, open terrain proved beneficial to Alexander's forces, but the Persian cavalry was still able to inflict devastating losses. Nevertheless, Alexander's forces were able to finally break through the Persian lines, and not only that, Alexander managed to make contact with Darius himself. The two began to clash openly with each other.

Alexander's leg was injured in the fray before they both tumbled to the ground and fought hand to hand. Darius, knowing that the battle was lost, is said to have "torn off his royal robes" and retreated with the remnant of his forces. But in his haste, he did not bring his own wife and mother with him. Even though his advisors had warned him against bringing members of the royal family to the fight, Darius had brought them regardless.

He would regret it. Now, Alexander had two important royal hostages in his custody. Darius probably figured that Alexander was going to use them for leverage, but he never did. At one point, Darius even gave Alexander an extremely generous offer for a truce. Darius proclaimed that he would allow Alexander to keep all of the lands in Asia Minor that he was already in possession of, along with certain financial compensation and the hand of his daughter in marriage. Alexander could have all of this if he simply returned Darius's wife and mother to him unharmed.

However, Alexander revealed just how cold and callous he could be by refusing to enter into any negotiations. Instead, he headed farther south to the city of Tyre (in what is modern-day Lebanon) and besieged the city. The siege lasted for about seven months, but Alexander was ultimately victorious. During the siege, it is said that the city's defenders actually used a form of Greek fire on Alexander and his men.

This was essentially a sticky, napalm-like substance that was poured down from the city walls on top of Alexander and his troops. This terrible onslaught forced Alexander to make a tactical retreat. But it wasn't long before he and his military machine charged right back into place. This time around, they broke through the walls of Tyre and then laid waste to the city, killing some seven thousand of its residents.

After this rampage, Alexander went to Egypt, where he furthered his conquests, adding the Egyptians to his column and even founding a new city named after himself—Alexandria. This city would become a Greek metropolis and an international commercial hub of the Mediterranean. Alexander's next major campaign took him back up through Syria and then into what was then called Mesopotamia, which was a region comprised of parts of modern-day Syria, Turkey, Iraq, and Iran.

It was here, out on the Nineveh Plains in 331 BCE, that a climactic battle between the forces of Alexander and the Persian Empire would unfold. For this rematch, Darius had fielded an even larger force, greatly outnumbering Alexander's army. If Alexander had been your average person, he might have been kicking himself at this point for not accepting Darius's earlier generous offer for a truce since, for all intents and purposes, it looked as if all of the Macedonians were about to be annihilated.

But Alexander was not your average person. Even though he was greatly outnumbered, he pushed his army forward. By using an ingenious technique, he had his troops approach in a diagonal fashion so that the right flank would make contact with the Persian forces first. This allowed the Macedonian army the defensive advantage of collapsing into a protective square formation if the Persians threatened to surround them. The right flank could work like a battering ram against the Persian lines and then pull back to a defensive position when things became too much to handle.

Alexander himself led the decisive cavalry charge that broke through the enemy lines. Not only that, but Alexander also managed to launch an assault on Darius's own chariot. The driver was actually killed by one of Alexander's comrades, and in the confusion of the battle, many of the nearby Persians mistook the slain driver for being Darius. This caused great discord and distress in the Persian ranks, and some began to openly desert the fight, thinking that it was all over.

Darius, in the meantime, once again made a break for it, and he fled from the scene with whatever of his entourage he could get. At this point, Darius had basically lost control of his whole empire, and he was a man hunted, hounded, and in hiding. Alexander was able to step into just about any Persian capital and claim himself to be in control. A short time later, Alexander received an update on Darius. He learned that the Persian king had actually been usurped by a Persian general named Bessus, who was now claiming to be the new emperor.

Of course, Alexander could not allow such a challenge to go unopposed. He sent in his troops, and Bessus's forces were defeated. However, before they could reach Darius, he had already been fatally stabbed by Bessus. Alexander managed to see his old nemesis right before he expired. Although Alexander no doubt would have liked to have slain Darius himself, seeing him in such a pathetic state actually made the Macedonian feel sorry for him. In fact, he had Darius buried with full honors.

Alexander was now recognized as the new Persian emperor, as well as the titular king of several other countries and principalities. This was not enough for him, though, and he eventually pushed on into regions as far as Uzbekistan, Afghanistan, and even western India. Alexander is said to have wanted to push even farther east, but his own army threatened to revolt if he did so.

It was for this reason that Alexander finally decided to settle for the territories he had gained, and he began to consolidate his holdings. His number one goal now was to find a way to unify all of the Macedonians, Greeks, Persians, Mesopotamians, Egyptians, and the like into one coherent empire. These plans were interrupted, however, when Alexander came down with a terrible fever and perished in 323 BCE.

The man who could not be bested on the battlefield succumbed to a viral infection. With his death, his empire splintered into several factions. But even so, Greek culture had already spread far and wide, and thanks to Alexander, the world would never be quite the same again.

Chapter 8 – The Aftermath of Alexander's Empire and the Beginning of the Greco-Roman Civilization

"If something were brought about without an antecedent cause, it would be untrue that all things come about through fate. But if it is plausible that all events have an antecedent cause, what ground can be offered for not conceding that all things come about through fate?"

-Chrysippus

At the time of his death in 323 BCE, Alexander the Great had spread Greek culture far and wide. And in many ways, the seeds that he planted would eventually give rise to that later Hellenistic-inspired conglomeration of nations—the Roman Empire. In the immediate aftermath of Alexander's demise, however, what would have been his Pan-Hellenic empire fractured into what could be termed as being several different Hellenistic kingdoms, which were ruled by his generals.

It must be stressed that although the generals were themselves Macedonian, they adopted the Greek culture and typically had Greek officials in their administrations; most of them even ruled over sizeable Greek populations. The general who ruled over the largest piece of territory was a Macedonian man named Seleucus. He ended up controlling Persia and Syria, and it was from his name that the Seleucid dynasty sprung.

Another successful former general of Alexander's was Ptolemy. Ptolemy famously set up shop in Egypt and essentially became a Hellenized pharaoh, whose line would only end with the death of the famous Cleopatra in 30 BCE.

Antigonus, another one of Alexander's generals, o would eventually take control of Macedonia and much of Greece. After Alexander the Great's death, it was actually the fate of Macedonia that would be in the greatest dispute.

Before Alexander had died, he had taken a wife by the name of Roxanne. Roxanne was pregnant when Alexander perished in 323 BCE. Shortly after Alexander's death, Roxanne gave birth to a son who was Christened Alexander IV. Since this child was obviously not old enough to rule, a regent by the name of Perdiccas was placed in charge of the day-to-day affairs until Alexander IV came of age. Alexander IV, however, would only get to live to be thirteen years old, as he was brutally murdered in the summer of 309 BCE.

After much infighting, one of Alexander's old generals, Antigonus, finally managed to set up a successful successor state. Although Alexander's empire had splintered, the Greek kingdoms that emerged (at least when they weren't fighting with each other) developed great economic, commercial, and cultural ties with one another. The doors had been pried open for extensive trade. Wine from Syria, papyrus from Egypt, spices from India, and gold from Greece were all available commodities, and they were shipped back and forth between the kingdoms of this suddenly Hellenized world.

And it wasn't just goods that received traffic far and wide but also ideas. Greek philosophies, such as stoicism, cynicism, and epicureanism, were suddenly circulating to other regions. It seems that since the Greeks no longer had to focus so much on defending themselves since they were under the protection of Macedonia, it gave them much more time to think—and think they did. Greek philosophers set up whole schools of thought, and many of these ideas found a place within the halls of none other than the Great Library of Alexandria, which had become the decided repository of the Hellenistic knowledge that had thus far been accumulated.

The first of these Hellenized kingdoms to fall was the one founded by Antigonus, which revolved around Macedonia itself. This occurred during the time of Antigonus's grandson, who was also named Antigonus or, as it were, Antigonus II Gonatas. The Gonatas part of his name was actually a nickname that translates as "kneecap." The reason behind this odd nickname has been subsequently lost to history. At any rate, it was during Antigonus II Gonatas's reign that Greece suffered a massive invasion around 270 BCE by a band of roving Celts.

These invaders were successfully repulsed, and they were forced to flee to Anatolia, where they were brought to task by Pergamon, who was the Hellenistic potentate of the region. Pergamon exiled the defeated Celts to Galatia. Shortly after the Celtic invasion, Antigonus II Gonatas had to fend off an invasion sent by the neighboring Kingdom of Epirus. Epirus was ruled by King Pyrrhus, from whom the famed expression "Pyrrhic victory" comes. Gonatas stayed the course in Macedon until he died in 239 BCE.

Antigonus II Gonatas would be succeeded by his male heir, a son by the name of Demetrius II. Demetrius would then reign supreme over Macedon over the course of the next ten years. At the very end of his tenure as king, the kingdom began to splinter. Demetrius II was succeeded by his son Philip V. Philip II of

Macedon may have begun Macedonia's rise to prominence, but ironically enough, Philip V of Macedon reigned over its demise.

This was due to a growing power to the west—the Roman Republic. The Romans, with their capital in Italy, had previously waged war with their powerful Carthaginian neighbors in North Africa. In 201 BCE, the Romans successfully put the Carthaginians down. With their southern front clear, the Romans began to look toward their eastern frontier, and soon, Macedonia fell into their sights.

Rome desired conquest, and as it pertained to Macedonia, it certainly did not help matters that the king of the Macedonians, Philip V, had previously aligned himself with Carthage. The Romans used this as a pretext for a punitive expedition. This charge was led by Roman commander Quinctius Flamininus. Initially, the Macedonians were able to hold their own, engaging in a classic phalanx formation, but it did not take long for the Romans to break the Macedonians' lines.

With the Macedonian army defeated, Philip was forced to follow the directives of the Roman who had bested him. It came as some surprise, however, when the Roman commander directed the Macedonian ruler to grant autonomy to the Greek city-states that had been under his dominion. It is unclear what Flamininus thought this would accomplish, but it seems he opened up Pandora's box. For as soon as freedom was restored, the Greeks went back to their old ways of fighting amongst each other, and not only that, they also began waging war against the Romans who had just freed them.

Soon, the most rebellious of the Greeks—Sparta—was in open conflict with the forces of Flamininus. This Spartan rebellion was led by a man by the name of Nabis, who was going around Greek city-states and stirring up the local populaces with promises of land redistribution should they stage a successful revolt. Such tidings were particularly alarming for the senators of the Roman Republic since they were primarily made up of the landed elite. As such, any mention of a major redistribution of land was perceived as an enormous threat to the social order, and not just for Greece but also the rest of the Mediterranean.

In order to contain this revolutionary ferment, the Roman senators did not hesitate to authorize military action, and soon, Roman troops were in Sparta putting down the political uprising.

Philip, in the meantime, eventually managed to wrestle back control of Macedonia, but it was short-lived. After another climactic battle with the Romans in 167 BCE, the Romans were able to assert their dominance once again in the region.

Initially, Rome sought out a hands-off approach with the Greeks, but when it was clear that this would not be tenable, Rome increased the reach of its direct control. First, the northern portions of Greece were lumped together with Macedonia, and they were referred to as the Roman province of Macedonia. Soon after this, southern and central Greece were lumped together into what was termed the province of Achaea.

After Roman dominion was assured, the regular Roman citizens began to show up in Greek lands to do business with the Greeks. It is said that the island of Delos, in particular, was transformed into a great financial hub for business. Sadly enough, much of this business was in literal human capital since Delos had a large slave trade operation, in which as many as ten thousand slaves were trafficked out of Greece every single day. The signs of the affluent Romans that came here to do business are still evident in the form of ancient Roman villas, whose interiors are decorated with elaborate mosaic tiles.

The Romans were not always welcomed, however, and internal discord and rebellion were frequent occurrences. One of the most impressive rebellions against Rome occurred in 88 BCE when Mithridates, a Hellenized king who reigned over the Kingdom of Pontus on the southern shores of the Black Sea, began to strike out against Romans in the region. These acts inspired the neighboring

Greeks to commit likewise acts, and soon, Mithridates was viewed as their own personal champion of freedom.

However, this march to freedom wasn't a pretty one. When several Greek city-states rose up to throw off the yoke of their perceived oppressors, it is said that thousands of visiting Romans were caught completely unaware and were slaughtered. The Greeks would face a severe backlash, and in 84 BCE, Roman general Lucius Cornelius Sulla (better known simply as Sulla), with the full might of Rome behind him, marched over to the Aegean and crushed Mithridates's army. He then marched on Athens itself, taking the city by force.

Over the next few decades, both Greece and Rome would see great shifts in the political sands. A man named Julius Caesar would rise up as a leading figure of the Roman Republic only to be assassinated in 44 BCE. This would mark the end of the Roman Republic, and it was followed by a period of turmoil that would ultimately result in the birth of the Roman Empire around 30 BCE, which was headed by the first Roman emperor—Augustus.

Roman rule managed to bring an end to the constant infighting between Greek city-states. Now everyone was under the same Roman administration, and they more or less fell in line with what their Roman procurators asked of them. There was no more wondering what the hot-headed Thebans might do come spring or if Sparta would launch a sneak attack on Athens—all of this incessant fighting was a thing of the past under direct Roman control.

The peace and security that the Romans provided allowed the Greeks to not worry about the potential for outside conflict and instead focus internally on themselves. This allowed philosophy and intellectual endeavors to flourish once more. And the Romans, despite their conquest of the Hellenized world, seemed to genuinely respect Greek culture and philosophy, adopting much of it themselves.

It was this symbiosis that gave rise to what is often termed to be Greco-Roman sensibilities. The admiration of Greece was a common occurrence in Imperial Rome. And some Roman emperors, such as the infamous Nero, put Greece on the top of the list when it came to palaces outside of Rome to pay homage to. He may have gone down in history as a crazed and bloodthirsty tyrant, but Nero knew great culture when he saw it. In 66 CE, he famously visited the region to personally participate in Olympic-styled sports, theater, and musical performances. Nero being Nero, of course, would have always received the gold medal in the Olympics since anything less could have resulted in the execution of those giving out the awards!

Other Roman emperors, such as Marcus Aurelius, were deeply steeped in Greek philosophy. Emperor Aurelius was a fervent practitioner of stoicism, the Greek philosophy that stresses self-control and moderation. But, of course, the biggest and most defining influence to hit the Greek-speaking world during the Pax Romana ("Roman Peace") wouldn't be stoicism, cynicism, or epicureanism; instead, it would be a new strain of Judaism imported from the Middle East called Christianity.

Chapter 9 – Christianity in the Greek-Speaking World

"For I choose to follow not men or men's doctrines, but God and the doctrines [delivered] by Him. For if you have fallen in with some who are called Christians, but who do not admit this [truth], and venture to blaspheme the God of Abraham, and the God of Isaac, and the God of Jacob; who say there is no resurrection of the dead, and that their souls, when they die are taken to heaven; do not imagine that they are Christians."

-Justin Martyr

Greece had always been a crossroads of ideas. Having said that, it is only natural that a vibrant new religion called Christianity might eventually make the rounds. Leading this charge was Paul the Apostle, who toured a string of Greek communities around 50 CE. Before we get into Paul's ministry in the Greek-speaking world, let us delve into his background a little bit.

Paul, who in his early life went by Saul, was born in a Hellenized Jewish community in Tarsus. He grew up with his foot in two worlds—that of the Hellenized Greeks and that of traditional Jewish culture and belief. Paul was a serious student of the Torah from a young age, and immediately after his bar mitzvah, he trained under the pharisaical Rabbi Gamaliel. He became a zealous believer in rabbinical law and sought to stamp out any deviation from Judaism. So, when Christianity became popular in Jerusalem, Paul looked at the nascent movement with worry and concern. And soon enough, he was moved to try and stamp it out, lest all of Israel became infected with what he viewed as false teachings.

In his passion to drive the Christians out, Paul became relentless in his persecution of them. According to New Testament scripture, he even stood watch while one of the apostles—Steven—was stoned to death. According to the Bible, Paul then made a trip to Damascus, Syria, with the intention of rooting out Christian gatherings that had formed there. It was on the road to Damascus that Paul allegedly encountered the supernatural. He later claimed to have seen a vision of a radiant light in the middle of the road, from which a voice inquired, "Saul! Saul! Why do you persecute me?" Paul asked, "Who are you, Lord?" At which the figure is said to have replied, "I am Jesus, whom you are persecuting." Without getting into too much of the details of Paul's visionary experience, it was after this road to Damascus moment that Saul the persecutor changed his name to Paul and went from persecuting Christians to being the most active spreader of the gospel. Of course, there are those who might debate the merits of the accounts in the New Testament, but as far as history goes (as well as Paul's letters stating the same), it was this moment that changed Paul's life forever.

And now that we have briefly looked at Paul's background and what allegedly led him to become a missionary, let us delve into his missionary exploits in the Greek-speaking world. Paul's first major mission abroad was actually in the city of Antioch in Anatolia. From here, he departed to Cyprus. In Cyprus, Paul and his fellow missionary Barnabas stopped at Salamis before heading to the Greek city of Paphos. It was in Paphos that Paul had a rather interesting encounter with a man named Bar-Jesus.

In the Jewish world, the name "Jesus" was actually a variation of Joshua. The name itself was not unusual. And the Hebrew prefix of "Bar" simply means son. So, someone named "Bar-Jesus" would literally be someone known as "Son of Jesus." Despite the similarity of his name, this man was nothing at all like Jesus Christ. In fact, it was said that he was a "sorcerer" and that he viciously heckled Paul at one of his speaking engagements.

According to the Book of Acts in the New Testament, Paul eventually grew so sick of the harassment that he shouted at the man, "You son of the devil, full of every sort of deceit and fraud, and enemy of all that is good! Will you never stop preventing the true ways of the Lord?" Paul then followed up his outrage with one of the few times that an apostle actually cursed someone. For it is said he shouted at the troublemaker, "Watch now, for the Lord has laid his hand of punishment upon you, and you will be struck blind, you will not see sunlight for some time." And sure enough, at least according to the biblical narrative, the man went blind.

Besides blinding folks, scripture tells us that Paul was able to get many of the local Greek-speaking population to convert to Christianity. Paul then headed back to Anatolia, where he ended up at the Greek settlement of Perga. Paul was once again able to spread his message to the populace, and many became acquainted with Christianity. Paul then went to the nearby Greek settlement of Iconium, and once again, Paul was well received. However, due to antagonism by local authority figures, he wrapped things up rather quickly before heading over to the settlement of Lystra.

Here, scripture tells us that Paul managed to heal a man who was unable to walk. Upon seeing this miracle, the Greeks who were present began to proclaim in astonishment that Paul and his partner Barnabas were gods. Yes, you heard that right; instead of considering the men as being messengers of the divine, their Greek audience was convinced that Paul and Barnabas themselves were divine beings. And as they talked amongst themselves in astonishment, they insisted that Paul must be a manifestation of Hermes and Barnabas a manifestation of Zeus.

As one might imagine, Paul was not too pleased with this sudden turn of events. As the crowd began to admire him and Barnabas in worshipful reverence, a disturbed Paul rebuked their efforts. He shouted at them, "Men—why are you doing these things? We also are men, of like nature with you, and we bring you good news, that you should turn from these vain things to a living God, who made the heaven and the earth and the sea and all that is in them."

At this point, Paul had only visited Greek settlements on the periphery of the Greek world, but around 50 CE, he left for Athens in Greece proper. It is said that Paul immediately immersed himself in the great discussions of religion and philosophy that were constantly bubbling to the surface in this intellectual cauldron. In particular, he showed up at a place called Mars Hill, where people participated in open discussions about all manner of metaphysical topics. On this hill, Paul famously addressed a crowd with the words, "Men of Athens, I notice that you are religious in every way, for as I was walking along, I saw your many shrines. And one of your altars had the inscription on it: 'To an Unknown God.' This God, whom you worship without knowing, is the one I am telling you about."

Paul was very smart in his approach. He was in the midst of all sorts of pagan worship, with idols and shrines set up to just about every deity conceivable. It was the Greek custom at the time to leave an additional shrine out to the so-called "unknown god" that they might have forgotten about. It was not really done with too much thought; really, it was just an afterthought to ensure that the Greeks had all of their metaphysical bases covered.

However, Paul used it to his advantage to break the ice with them and state that the unknown god they were worshiping was actually the God of whom he spoke. Paul then showed just how erudite he was when it came to Greek philosophy by seamlessly tying the words of a famous Greek poet with his own biblical beliefs. Paul stated, "He is the God who made the world and everything in it. Since He is the Lord of heaven and earth, He doesn't live in man-made temples, and human hands cannot serve His needs, for He has no needs. He himself gives life and breath to everything, and He satisfies every need. From one man He created all the nations throughout the whole earth. He decided beforehand when they should rise and fall, and He determined their boundaries. His purpose was for the nations to seek after God and perhaps feel their way toward Him and find Him though He is not far from any of us. For in Him we live and move and exist. As some of your own poets said, 'We are his offspring.'"

Paul was actually quoting the words of the Stoic philosopher Aratus of Soli, who, in his philosophical treatise, "Phaenomena," described his views on the nature of the universe and humanity as the offspring of divinity. Paul had also paraphrased the words of another Greek philosopher, Epimenides. Paul borrowed from him the words, "For in him we live and move and have our being."

Epimenides had actually written those words about the Greek god Zeus. He wrote them at a time when many Greeks were casting away their belief in the old gods as if they had buried them in a tomb. The full quote from Epimenides actually reads, "They fashioned a tomb for you, holy and high one, Cretans, always liars, evil beasts, idle bellies. But you are not dead: you live and abide forever. For in you we live and move and have our being."

But even though Epimenides wrote this about Zeus, anyone familiar with Christianity can see the parallels to Christian thought since Christians believe that Jesus was buried in a tomb only to be resurrected and "live and abide forever" after the third day. And Paul no doubt had Jesus in mind when he thought of the words of this Greek poet, simply substituting Zeus for Jesus.

Paul's preaching in Greece was indeed successful, and several local churches began to take root. However, these early churches had to remain underground since local authorities often frowned upon the new religion. In its early beginnings, Christianity was largely misunderstood for a variety of reasons. The practice of communion, for example, in which Christians passed around wine and bread and repeated the words of Christ, "This is my blood. This is my body." had Christian believers being accused of cannibalism.

Christians were so secretive in the early days—much of this secrecy borne out of necessity—that these common misunderstandings turned into gross exaggerations. The early church in Greece faced a vicious cycle of having to be secretive in order to avoid persecution, only for this very secrecy to produce further gossip about them and further misunderstandings of the faith. This led to the rise of many so-called Christian apologists, who would attempt to explain and argue extensively about the true nature of the Christian faith, the most famous of which was Justin Martyr.

Justin was born around 100 CE in the region of Samaria in northern Israel. Justin was actually of Greek origin, although he grew up around Samaritan culture. Early on in life, he immersed himself in Greek philosophy, but he was unable to answer certain philosophical questions, so he turned to Christianity. Justin Martyr wrote lengthy apologetic texts, attempting to explain his reasoning for converting to Christianity until he was beheaded in 165 CE.

Christianity would continue to suffer from various waves of persecution until Roman Emperor Constantine issued the Edict of Milan in 313 CE, which officially "legalized" Christianity. This edict allowed Christians to come out into the open and practice their faith without fear of repercussions. From this point forward, Christians in Greece and much of the rest of the Roman Empire would flourish.

Soon, rather than merely being tolerated as an acceptable religion, Christianity would become the official religion of the empire itself. Emperor Constantine would also eventually become a Christian. He would also establish a new Christianized capital for the Roman Empire, not in the Latin West but in the Greek East, on the grounds of the old Greek settlement of Byzantium, which was located on a narrow strip of land that connected the European continent to Asia Minor (Turkey).

Once the old site of Byzantium was rendered into the new Roman capital, it was renamed in honor of Constantine himself; it was called Constantinople. As good as all these things were for Christians, the fact that Christianity had suddenly become the main religion of the Roman Empire kick-started a major ideological shift among the faithful.

In the past, when Christians were horribly persecuted by Roman authorities, it was widely believed among Christians that the Roman Empire would soon face God's wrath. It was a common belief that Rome would be destroyed in the events of Armageddon mentioned in the Christian Book of Revelation. But once the Roman Empire itself became Christian, it obviously caused many Christians to second-guess that assumption. However, it would not be long before Christians would look elsewhere for potential harbingers of the apocalypse.

Chapter 10 – The Rise and Fall of the Greek Byzantine Empire

"You see that even the enemy did not dare to declare war against us until they had seized our generals, for they were sensible that, while we had commanders and yielded obedience to them, we were able to conquer them; but, having seized our commanders, they concluded that we should, from a want of command and discipline, be destroyed."

-Xenophon

The Roman Empire, in many ways, had become too big for its own good. And under its top-down authoritarian regimes, the ever-expanding territory of the Roman Empire had become increasingly hard for one Roman emperor to govern. Constantine had successfully ruled the Roman Empire as the sole emperor, but his successors would not be quite as capable. And by 395 CE, the Roman Empire was once again split in two, with one emperor ruling the Greek East while the other ruled the Latin West.

The western half of the Roman Empire was frequently besieged by roving bands of Germanic tribes, such as the Ostrogoths, Visigoths, Franks, and Vandals. As the name of the Germanic Vandals might imply, these aggressive warriors specialized in smash-

and-grab tactics of attacking, looting, and fleeing. Initially, the Romans were able to stand up to the incursions, but over time, the constant fighting finally broke Rome's back, and the western half of the Roman Empire ended in 476 CE.

The eastern, Greek portion of the Roman Empire based out of Constantinople would go on to last another one thousand years, and it would be rechristened the Byzantine Empire. As the Western half of the Roman Empire lay in ruins, the eastern half would remain strong with a series of successful emperors, as well as a powerful Greek Orthodox Church apparatus. Similar to the Western Roman Empire's development of Catholicism and the pope in Rome, the Byzantines would establish the office of the patriarch in Constantinople for their top bishop, who is often referred to in the Orthodox faith as the "first among equals."

In the immediate aftermath of the Western Roman Empire's fall, the Greek half of the empire was primarily on the defense, fending off and sometimes bribing troublemakers who were threatening their borders. It was not until the reign of Byzantine Emperor Justinian I (also known as Justinian the Great) that the Greek half of the empire sought to reclaim some of the lands that had been lost. Justinian rose to the Byzantine throne in 527, and he wasted no time on embarking upon his plan of *renovatio imperii Romanorum,* or as it were, the "restoration of the empire of the Romans."

In order to do so, however, Justinian knew that he had to placate his greatest threat to the east—Persia—so that he would be able to focus the full might of his forces in the west. It was with this express purpose in mind that Justinian came to terms with Persian King Khosrow in 532. The terms of the agreement were not that great since it entailed the Byzantines having to pay tribute to the Persians, but it was enough to get them off of their backs, allowing them to focus on reclaiming the lost lands of the Western Roman Empire.

But before Justinian could focus on his project of reclamation, he also had to ensure the stability of his own capital. For in that very year, Justinian had to put down the so-called Nika riots. In order to understand the Nika riots, one must understand the popularity of chariot racing in the Roman world. The Greek East had created a tremendous pastime in which spectators watched teams of chariots competing against each other. These teams were known by colors associated, and by the time of Justinian, the two most prominent teams were the Greens and the Blues.

These teams represented more than just sports; they also represented political and even military power. The Blues had powerful backers, and so did the Greens. These two teams were usually opposed to each other, but in light of Justinian's sudden taxing of his citizens to fund his impending conquest, as well as his decision to pay tribute to the Persians, they actually joined forces to show their disdain.

This popular uprising broke loose during a chariot race in which Justinian was in attendance. During the course of the races, spectators began to shout, "Nika! Nika!" over and over. The word "Nika" means "victory." This word was shouted in between angry remarks made about Justinian himself. In this hostile atmosphere, thousands of Greeks came out onto the street to attempt an outright overthrow of the government. Emperor Justinian was understandably shocked at these developments, but he regained his senses fast enough and sent in troops to quell the unrest. He was indeed able to restore order, but it has been estimated that tens of thousands were killed in the ensuing melee.

So, after the eastern frontier was stabilized and his own people were under control, Justinian began to send his Greek forces into the former Western Roman Empire to retake lands that had been conquered. First, he sent an army led by Byzantine general Belisarius to take back territory in North Africa, which the Vandals had seized in 429 CE. The territory was reclaimed with relative ease. General Belisarius then turned north and managed to capture the southern Italian town of Naples before marching on Rome itself.

By the 550s, the Byzantines had managed to reclaim much of the former western portion of the Roman Empire. Justinian's territory stretched through the Middle East, all across North Africa, to southern Spain and a smattering of Mediterranean islands, leading to the reclaimed Italian Peninsula and then back to the Greek heartland itself. But Justinian's successors would steadily lose this reclaimed territory.

In fact, his immediate successor, Justin II, lost most of Italy to an invasion of the Lombards—a Germanic tribe that would control almost the entire Italian Peninsula for the next two centuries. Justinian II was followed by Byzantine Emperor Tiberius II, who ended up fighting a losing battle against Slavic invasions of the Greek Balkan territory. It was around this time that the people groups of the Slavs, Avars, Patzinaks, and Bulgars, in particular, began to appear in the Greek territory.

The next emperor, Maurice, found a unique way to solve the problem of the Balkans. The old Byzantine foe of Persia had erupted into a civil war, prompting the Byzantines to intervene. Maurice was able to successfully put his thumb on the scale, and he tipped it in favor of Khosrow II. Khosrow thanked the Byzantine emperor, which led to closer relations. Emperor Maurice even married the Persian king's daughter, shoring up relations even further. With the Persians suddenly in the Byzantine's back pocket, Maurice could finally focus on driving out the Byzantines' enemies from the Balkans—a feat that was achieved in 602 CE.

You might think that Emperor Maurice would be loved by his Greek subjects for his success, but due to the fact that the Slavic Avars had stolen thousands of Greek citizens, with Maurice essentially ignoring this, he was not particularly popular. Dissension broke out in the ranks, and a Byzantine soldier, whose name comes down to us as Phocas, led a rebellion on the capital and had the emperor killed.

Phocas turned out to be even less popular than Maurice, and he could not escape the stigma of being seen as a usurper to the throne. Complicating matters for him was the fact that the Persian king now considered all the previous treaties null and void since Phocas had assassinated his former brother-in-law.

Phocas was ultimately removed from power by a popular Byzantine general named Heraclius in 610. Right around the time that Heraclius came to power, a prophet by the name of Muhammad had begun his ministry in the lands of Arabia. At the time, he was just one lone figure, slowly gathering a following of like-minded believers. But one day, Muhammad's successors would build up an army that would march on Constantinople itself.

However, during Heraclius's reign, the number one threat to Byzantium would remain the Persian Empire. In fact, shortly after Heraclius came to the throne, the Persian forces stormed into the Byzantine territory in the Middle East, seizing both the cities of Jerusalem and Damascus. Heraclius was able to rally his forces, and during the Battle of Nineveh in 627, he was able to soundly defeat the Persians.

The Byzantines managed to reclaim the territory they had lost, but both the Byzantine Empire and the Persian Empire had fought each other to a standstill as a result. This led to both empires becoming significantly weakened. And it was during this moment of weakness that the Muslim armies began to rise up and chip away at both of these former juggernauts. Muhammad, at this time, had successfully taken over all of the Arabian Peninsula (modern-day Saudi Arabia, Yemen, United Arab Emirates, Qatar, and Oman).

With this power base secure, the forces of Islam began to threaten Byzantine holdings. The first major confrontation occurred in 629 at the Battle of Mu'tah, which took place at the selfsame village of Mu'tah just to the east of the Jordan River. This opening battle did not go well for the Muslim fighters, and the Byzantines were easily able to drive them out. Not only that, three important Muslim military commanders were killed, one after the other. This was a terrible defeat for Muhammad's forces, but it would not be enough to deter him or his followers.

The Battle of Yarmouk in the borderlands of Syria and Jordan would prove to be a decisive one. Muhammad had already passed away at this point, having died in the summer of 632. His successors, however, would carry on the fight for him, and zealous jihadists scored a decisive victory against the Byzantines in 636. In a matter of decades, all of Palestine was in Muslim hands, which allowed the Islamic armies to permanently station themselves in Syria.

From this base, these warriors would send further incursions into the Byzantine heartland of Anatolia and threaten the Greek Byzantine capital of Constantinople. The city was besieged from 674 to 678. The Greeks were ultimately able to repel the Muslims by using the secret art of Greek fire. Although some minor raids would continue to occur off and on, this victory managed to keep major onslaughts at bay. It was not until 717 that Islamic forces would once again try their luck with a direct attack on Constantinople.

A combination of factors helped the Byzantines drive off this latest incursion. Sure, Greek fire was employed, but so was a whole lot of diplomacy with the Bulgar tribes that had settled in the Balkan region today known as Bulgaria. The newly allied Bulgars were a great help in augmenting the Byzantines' might. Even the weather proved to be favorable for a Byzantine victory since the stormy conditions nearly wiped out their opponents' ships.

It was really this victory that bought the Byzantine Empire some much-needed time, as it resulted in the Muslim caliphate changing its aims and looking elsewhere for territorial gains. The Byzantines, in the meantime, began to question if perhaps they had fallen out of

God's favor. Interestingly enough, they began to consider the fact that the Muslims eschewed all manner of icons, as they refused to have any paintings of religious figures, no matter their importance. This is the reason why there are few depictions of Prophet Muhammad. Muslims did this because they felt that paintings of religious figures took focus away from God (Allah) and actually amounted to a form of idolatry.

Somewhere along the way, some leading thinkers in the Byzantine Empire began to wonder if God was, in fact, displeased with the Byzantine habit of having rich and elaborate religious icons. These sentiments kick-started a religious struggle that took place from 726 to 842. This was a pitched ideological battle between those who revered the religious icons of the Greek Orthodox faith and those who wished to see them removed. The Greeks were always known for their artwork, so, of course, Christian Byzantium was full of all kinds of religious works of art, including grand mosaics of religious scenes, sculptures, and other religious icons.

But as mentioned, those who were against the icons—the so-called iconoclasts—wished to have these revered works of art removed as quickly as possible. It is said that it was mostly the non-Greek residents of the far eastern regions who had to deal with Muslim incursions who were the most opposed to the icons, whereas the much more integrated Greeks tended to embrace them.

But no matter what side of the debate the Byzantines fell under, the rising tide of Islam still battered against its shores. By 900 CE, much of the Byzantines' frontier regions were lost. They lost their grip of Sicily in 902, and they nearly lost Thessaloniki in 904. Over the next couple of centuries, the situation would look increasingly dire for the Byzantines. It was so bad, in fact, that by the 1090s, the Byzantines began to seek help from the pope in Rome, even though the pope had previously excommunicated the Greek Orthodox patriarch due to doctrinal differences.

At this point in time, the Germanic tribes that had succeeded the Western Roman Empire had melded with the remnants of the Romans to form the medieval kingdoms of western Europe. As the medieval Europeans grew stronger, the once-mighty Byzantines were growing weaker until they were actively seeking out help from the westerners. This, along with accounts of Christian pilgrims being harassed in the Holy Land, is what led Pope Urban II to call for the First Crusade.

Christians in the west readily answered this call, and soon, European armies were sent crashing into Muslim forces in the Middle East. The First Crusade managed to wrest much of the Holy Land from the grasp of the Islamic power brokers of the region. But over the next two centuries, these gains were steadily reversed, and by 1291, the last of the Christian Crusaders had been expelled from the Middle East.

This left the Byzantine Empire once again alone on the front lines, facing off against an ever-expanding Muslim force. And soon enough, the latest Muslim power to gain prominence—the Ottoman Turks—would prove to be the Byzantines' undoing. The Byzantine Empire ultimately fell to the Ottomans in 1453 after a prolonged siege that saw the Ottoman Turks blasting the great walls of the city with powerful cannons.

Even faced with this onslaught, the Byzantines managed to hold off the Turks for about two months. The walls of Constantinople were thick and strong, and the fact that they withstood the Turks' firepower for several weeks is a testament to that. The sultan's cannons were cumbersome and time-consuming to reload, so during those breaks in between firing and reloading, the Greeks did everything they could to repair any damage that had been inflicted.

Nevertheless, the Turks did indeed eventually break through the walls of Constantinople, and by all accounts, what happened next was a terrible bloodbath. The Greeks were greatly outnumbered by the invaders, and despite the many acts of heroism that were displayed that day, they were quickly overrun by the Turks. It is said that Byzantine Emperor Constantine XI Palaeologus (it is perhaps ironic that the last Byzantine emperor shared the same name as the first) personally led the last desperate charge against the Ottomans, perishing in the onslaught.

With the defeat of the Byzantine troops, the Greek citizens of the city were massacred, tortured, and horribly abused at the hands of their enemies. Neither priests, nuns, nor small children were spared. Thousands of residents were enslaved. The rape and pillage of Constantinople went on for three whole days until Ottoman Sultan Mehmed II ordered a cessation of the violence.

An eyewitness to this devastation comes down to us from a man known to history as Leonard of Chios. Chios, of course, was a Greek island within the Byzantine Empire, from which Leonard had hailed. Leonard was a Greek scholar, and he was apparently in Constantinople that day and somehow managed to live to tell of the horrors he saw.

Leonard reported, "All the valuables and other booty were taken to their [the Turks] camp, and as many as sixty thousand Christians who had been captured. The crosses which had been placed on the roofs or the walls of churches were torn down and trampled. Women were raped, virgins deflowered and youths forced to take part in shameful obscenities. The nuns left behind, even those who were obviously such, were disgraced with foul debaucheries."

In the aftermath, even the great Christian Orthodox church, the Hagia Sophia, would be transformed, although it would not be destroyed. Still, many Greek Christians saw the act of transforming the church as a defilement, as the conquerors of Constantinople converted it into a mosque. This towering piece of Byzantine architecture would now be accompanied by minarets, which were installed by the Ottoman Turks.

After the dissolution of the Ottoman Empire, the Hagia Sophia was later turned into a museum. But in recent years, hard-liners in Turkey have called for it to be reconverted back into a mosque. This would be a controversial move for sure since such an act would most certainly open up the old wounds of the past.

At any rate, after over one thousand years, the great Christian empire of Byzantium had fallen. Constantinople, the imperial capital of Christianity, would become Istanbul, Turkey. All of Christian Europe was shocked to hear of these developments. The loss of this Christian bulwark in the east sent a seismic shift throughout all of Christian Europe, but none were affected more than Greece itself, which was essentially now on the front lines of the Muslim advance. With Constantinople gone, many feared that Athens would be next.

Chapter 11 – The Struggle for Greek Independence

"Cut away all that is excessive, straighten all that is crooked, bring light to all that is overcast, labor to make all one glow of beauty and never cease chiseling your statue, until there shall shine out on you from it the godlike splendor of virtue, until you shall see the perfect goodness surely established in the stainless shrine."

-Plotinus

The capital of the Byzantine Empire was overrun by Ottoman forces in 1453, leaving Greece itself wide open to invasion. Only the so-called Despotate of the Morea, which made up most of the Peloponnese of southern Greece, was left. It was the last outpost of the former Byzantine Empire. Defenders of this land fought hard to fend off the Ottomans, but it proved to be an impossible task.

Athens fell to the Ottomans just five short years later, in 1458. The cradle of Western civilization was now officially in the possession of the east, and the rest of the Peloponnese would follow by 1460. As destructive as the Turkish military was and as horrible as the bloodthirsty pillaging of Constantinople, in particular, had been, the rule of the Ottomans was in some ways surprisingly benevolent, especially when it came to the Christian clergy.

The conquering sultan of Byzantium, Mehmed II, officially appointed a new patriarch in Constantinople, who was a Greek named Gennadius II, in 1454. It is said that at the patriarch's swearing-in ceremony that the sultan urged him to "be Patriarch, and good fortune be with you. Count on our friendship in whatever you will, possessing all those privileges which the Patriarchs enjoyed before you."

Many conquering Muslims were willing, to some extent, to follow the precepts of the Quran as it pertained to Christians and Jews. The Quran (also spelled as Koran, the central religious text of Islam) refers to Christians as people of the book and advises Muslims to treat them well as long as they pay a tax to Muslim authorities. Yes, Christians essentially had to pay a protection racket to stay safe. They were essentially considered to be second-class citizens, but the terms were more favorable than many would-be Christian conquerors would have dictated.

After all, Christian kingdoms during this period were likely to demand subject people immediately convert to Christianity. The Muslims, on the other hand, gave the conquered people a choice to either convert to Islam or retain their original faith and pay a special tax called jizya. But money was not the only thing that the Turks taxed. Shockingly enough, they also demanded a tax of children, as they required Greek families offer up one of their boys to be taken and raised by the Ottomans and groomed for a special military auxiliary force called the Janissaries.

In Turkish, this practice was called devshirme, but for the Greeks, it was known as *pedhomazoma* or "child collection." These young boys were brought up to be fierce fighters for the Ottomans. They actively fought for Islam and were made to be zealous believers in the faith. One can only imagine the agony of their Greek Orthodox parents in having to deal with all of this.

However, not all of the kidnapped boys became fighting men, as some were trained in more specialized tasks. Some even reached high administrative positions within the Ottoman government. According to one account, a Greek child by the name of Sinan was carried off by the Ottomans in 1491. He was raised in "palace schools" and ultimately succeeded in becoming the chief architect of the empire, building colossal structures. Some of his works are indeed perceived to be the best achievements of Ottoman architecture. But the individual who designed and built them was not Turkish but rather a transplanted Greek ripped from his family in his youth and made to serve the Ottoman Empire.

The Ottomans divided up Greece into six districts, with each one governed by a local administrator who was loyal to the sultan. Even though the Ottomans controlled Greece, there remained pockets of unruly resistance in Greece's mountainous terrain. These rebels would periodically rise up against the Ottomans, but the damage done to the regime was always minimal.

A few other outliers of resistance remained, but they were steadily pushed back. In 1522, the Ottomans besieged the island of Rhodes in the eastern Mediterranean, driving out the Knights Hospitaller—a vestige of the Crusades—who had been stationed there. The Greek island of Cyprus, which at this point was controlled by the Republic of Venice, held out for a while too, but it was ultimately taken by the Ottomans in 1579. It was only by virtue of the Republic of Venice and its control of the Ionian Islands that enabled any portion of Greek-speaking lands to be free of Ottoman domination.

Some Greeks accepted their fate of being under Ottoman dominion, but others, especially in the rural mountainous regions, kept up periodic resistance throughout Ottoman rule. Others took advantage of the situation and moved to the more cosmopolitan cities of western Asia Minor, such as Constantinople and Smyrna. Here, skilled Greeks could often make a lot of money by gaining work as merchants and administrators. Those who did not wish to be under the Ottoman yoke, however, also had the choice to flee. And many decided to depart their ancestral homes for western Europe.

Italy, in particular, received a large influx of Greek refugees. This sudden deposit of Greek culture in Italy would eventually germinate into the intellectual movement known as the Renaissance. It was the sparks set by the transplanted Greek intelligentsia that sparked this thirst for knowledge in the west. But even as the west became enriched by this influx of Greek refugees, Greece itself became increasingly backward and poor. Greece's industry suffered, and what little money the people had was taxed by the Ottomans.

As historian David Brewer put it, the Greeks were subject to "increasingly complex, arbitrary, and oppressive taxes." They were taxed for farms, vineyards, and even the raising of sheep—all of this on top of the general jizya tax that had to be paid simply to exist as Greek Orthodox Christians in the Ottoman Empire. By the 1600s, Greece had been reduced to an impoverished state, and many Greek towns saw a rapid decrease in population, which was brought about by those fleeing the harsh economic conditions that were being imposed.

During these dark times, the citizens of Greece clung to the Greek Orthodox faith. For the Greeks, their religion was everything, and thankfully enough, their Muslim overlords did not take it away from them. Although non-Muslims were forced to pay a tax for the continuation of their faith, they were mostly allowed to adhere to their religious beliefs. The hardest part of Greek life under Ottoman rule, no doubt, was the fact that the Ottomans could come and take a Greek family's children at any time.

As mentioned above, boys could be groomed for service in either the military or an administrative position. Many Greek young men made up an entire legion of the Ottoman army known as the Janissaries. These young men would be raised to be religious fanatics, and they would often return home to pressure their former families to convert to Islam just as they had. But as bad as things were for Greek boys, they were perhaps far worse for Greek girls. If the Ottomans so pleased, Greek girls could be snatched up and placed in harems. As romantic as such things were sometimes made out to be, this was nothing short of sexual slavery being imposed upon Greek women and girls.

There were some instances in which the Greeks refused to hand over their children to the Turks. One of the most notable incidents occurred in 1705 when a Turkish administrator came to northern Greece to collect fifty boys for the Janissaries. The administrator was immediately met with a hostile crowd of parents who began defiantly insisting that under no circumstances would they hand over their children. Rather than turn over their sons, the crowd mobbed the administrator and killed him on the spot. As bold as their resistance was, it was not long before Turkish retribution visited them. As a result, all who were involved in this resistance were rounded up and beheaded.

There have been some Ottoman apologists that have tried to downplay these abuses in later years, but no matter how one might try to sugarcoat it, life under the Ottoman rule was often not a very happy one for the Greeks. Despite the dark clouds hovering over the Greeks, by the 1750s, the illumination of the Enlightenment of western Europe began to make its way over to Greece. Soon, Greek translations of the works of Rousseau, Montesquieu, and Voltaire were surfacing in Greek cities.

The latter of which gave the Greeks the most hope since Voltaire was himself a lover of Greek civilization, and he openly encouraged the European powers to intervene on Greece's behalf. In 1770, Voltaire even pleaded with Greece's powerful fellow Orthodox nation to the north, Russia, to directly aid in the liberation of Greece. Russia's Catherine the Great did attempt as much after the outbreak of the Russo-Turkish War, which took place between 1768 and 1774.

This war was initiated due to hostilities between the Polish and the Ottomans. As the situation escalated, Russian troops parked themselves in the borderland between Poland and the nearest reaches of the Ottoman Empire. The war ultimately proved to be a great success for a resurgent Russia. The Russians managed to gain territory in the Caucasus region, and Romania, Serbia, and Montenegro achieved liberation. In the backdrop of all of this, Empress Catherine the Great sent Russian diplomats to Greece to engage in secret discussions about staging a revolt against the Ottomans, pledging Russian support for the Greeks.

The Russian Navy, under the leadership of Alexei Orlov, arrived off the shores of Mani in southern Greece in February of 1770. The turnout of Greek rebels was lower than expected, with less than two thousand participating. Soon, extra help arrived from Crete, and the Greek rebels were able to go on the offensive against the Ottomans. This resulted in Ottoman troops being pushed out of the regions of Laconia and Morea, but soon after that, the offensive stalled.

However, the worst was yet to come. As soon as word of these developments reached the ears of the Ottoman sultan, the Ottoman Empire engaged in a punishment of the worst kind against all Greeks throughout the empire. Whether they had participated in any revolutionary activity or not, every Greek resident of the Ottoman Empire was suddenly subject to persecution, abuse, and quite possibly death for no other reason than the fact that they were Greek.

This "anti-Greek pogrom," as it were, was enough to frighten the Greeks into submission. But as bad as things were, it was not a complete disaster for the Greeks. For after the Russians won the war and concluded a treaty with the Ottomans, the Ottoman Empire pledged to allow the Russians to place Greek Orthodox Christians and churches under Russian protection. It was a rather vague sense of protection, especially in the aftermath of the massacre the Turks had just finished against the Greeks, but the idea that a great power such as Russia was officially taking the Greeks into consideration meant a lot at the time.

At any rate, it was this nascent rebellion that planted the seeds of what would ultimately become the Greek War of Independence several decades later. By the late 1700s, both the French and American Revolutions were able to serve as an inspiration for a similar Greek revolt. And the mindset that was developing in the Greek intelligentsia was made clear in 1806 when a Greek patriot penned an anonymous treatise entitled, *The Rule of Law for Greece: A Discourse on Freedom.*

The paper expounds upon the Enlightenment thinker Jean-Jacques Rousseau's concept of man's original nature being one of "primitive happiness" and that it was only the contrivances of oppressive social structures that had robbed man of his joy. The writer then argued that the tendency of humanity is always to improve the state that they are in. The treatise stated that since the Ottoman Empire was already in decline, the Greeks should be able to break free. It was reasoned that there were two main obstacles that prevented the Greeks from doing so, and they were the rich Greek merchants and the Greek Orthodox clergy. It was argued that rich Greek merchants were happy with the status quo and did not want to rock the boat, while the clergy was completely beholden to the Turks and unable to think for themselves.

Shortly after this work was circulated, the Greek Orthodox Church began to strike back, and it condemned these Enlightenment-inspired ideals as nothing short of sinful and something that would ultimately lead the Greek faithful astray. These feelings were best expressed in an encyclical issued in 1819 by Patriarch Gregory V, which was called "Enlightenment as the Handmaid of Irreligion."

Here, he argued that the so-called knowledge of the Enlightenment would only lead to irreligion and, as he phrased it, "false patriots" who were "unworthy of their ancestral calling." In other words, how much would the Greeks profit to gain the ideals being proffered upon them by the Western world if in so doing they compromise their traditions and lose their ancestral soul?

This was the argument being made by the Greek Orthodox Church at the time. Yes, they knew that the Turkish regime was horribly oppressive, but, as the treatise rightfully stated, they did not want to risk losing their faith in a pursuit of liberation. The Greek Orthodox Church had come to view the so-called progress of western Europe as a threat to old traditions and philosophical outlooks. By clinging to the old way of doing things, the Greek Orthodox faith influenced schooling, and it avoided the modern sciences of astronomy and mathematics in favor of teaching long, outdated musings by classic Greek titans such as Aristotle. Although the west certainly still revered Greek figures like Aristotle, it accepted that many of his theories were off-base and needed a more modern interpretation.

Aristotle, for example, did not understand gravity, and he spoke of rocks falling to the ground simply out of an innate desire to return to the earth, as well as flames of fire moving upward because they wished to return to the air. Aristotle believed that nature had a place for everything, and phenomena such as these were simply a result of objects returning to their natural place. Aristotle had no evidence to support this theory; it was basically just something he surmised from pure speculation. In the 1700s, Isaac Newton, of course, dispelled all of this nonsense with his mathematically proven theories of gravity. However, Greek schooling still embraced Aristotle's and other great ancient Greeks' teachings wholeheartedly, and as a result, Greece was behind its European counterparts.

As Greek-speaking people were debating the merits of old tradition and newfangled ideas, the movement for Greek independence suddenly received help from an unexpected source. Ali Pasha, the viceroy of Ioannina, was flirting with open rebellion from the Ottoman Empire.

Ali Pasha had expanded his control to include southern Albania, the Peloponnese, and much of western Greece. By 1812, Ali was in a powerful position, as he controlled the prosperous town of Ioannina, taking full advantage of its rock-solid economy. It was only in 1820 that it all came crashing down when the Ottomans decided to rein in the rebellious province. Ali was a crafty politician, and in order to thwart the Ottoman attempt to knock him back in line, he reached out to the Russians to recognize his domain as an autonomous region.

In exchange for this favor, he enacted several reforms that were favorable for the Greek populace. He reduced taxation, wrote off debts, and abolished enforced servitude. The Turks, in the meantime, were closing in on Ali Pasha, and by the fall of 1820, they had pushed deep into his territory. Everywhere they went, they burned down villages, terrorized Greek citizens, and generally left the place in ruins.

Ali Pasha was forced to escape to the citadel in Ioannina, and he prepared to dig in for a long siege. But if the Ottomans felt that they had restored order in the region, they had another thing coming. By the spring of 1821, all of Greece seemed to be in revolt. In February there was an uprising in the Danubian principalities of Wallachia and Moldavia led by a Russian officer who was originally of Greek extraction—Alexander Ypsilantis. Soon thereafter, the Greeks of the Peloponnese rose up and openly declared war.

The first major gains happened in the fall of 1821 when Greek rebels, led by one Theodoros Kolokotronis, started to besiege Tripolitsa. At the same time, Greek ships were put together and sent on a crash course to smash into the Ottoman Navy in the

Aegean Sea. This was crucial since it literally kept additional Ottoman troop arrivals at bay, preventing them from making landfall.

Back in the Peloponnese, the Turks were being completely driven out. A huge victory was scored on October 5th when the Greek rebels managed to take over Tripolitsa. The capture of this town was important since it consisted of the major administrative center for Ottoman control of the region. The dreadful massacre that ensued, however, was nothing short of terrible. It is said that tens of thousands of Turkish inhabitants of the city were put to death even after surrendering. Yes, as much as the Greeks had suffered for centuries under the Ottomans and had atrocities inflicted upon them by the Turks, Greek freedom fighters were not always immune to descending into murderous mayhem.

It is important to note that although some Greeks butchered Turks, it does not mean that all Greeks were responsible. Such a thing would seem like common sense, yet this logic was completely lost on the Turkish sultan when he heard of what had happened at Tripolitsa. Since Christian Greeks were involved, the sultan immediately blamed all Christian Greeks. The first thing he did, in fact, was have the Greek Orthodox patriarch of Constantinople killed; he was executed that Easter Sunday.

Even though the patriarch, who was in far off in Constantinople, had nothing to do with the rebellion in the Peloponnese—in fact, he had excommunicated those involved—the Turks held him responsible since he was the leader of the Greek Christians. Yes, even though the sultan gave the patriarch great privileges, the sultan could end his life at a moment's notice if he so desired. Yet another reason for the Greek Orthodox faithful to want to throw off the Turkish yoke.

After killing the patriarch, another mass persecution (if not outright mass extermination) of Greeks within the Ottoman Empire commenced. Prominent Greeks were grabbed up by mobs of Turks and killed on the spot in Smyrna, Adrianople, and Constantinople. In the city of Kydonies alone, it is said that about thirty thousand Greeks were killed. In the Greek communities in Rhodes, Kos, and Cyprus, the situation was even worse, with whole communities being annihilated.

Even more atrocities occurred on the island of Chios, in which thousands were decimated. Not only were they killed, but the killers were also depraved enough to desecrate their remains. They would take bags of human body parts back to Constantinople simply so they would have the pleasure of dumping them in the street. These outrages soon reached the ears of western Europe, and the European nations were in an uproar, with many rattling their sabers to aid Greece in its time of need.

Northern Greece, in the meantime, saw its gains rapidly rolled back by the Turkish forces. The rebels here were soon pushed south, where they linked up with the rebels in the Peloponnese. The besieged Ali Pasha met his end in January of 1822 when his compound was stormed by Turkish troops, although the exact details of his demise remain unclear.

With Pasha eliminated, Turkish troops headed south later that spring to put down the rebellion still brewing in the Peloponnese. Without direct outside aid and with tensions building among the rebels themselves, it seemed as if the Turks were poised to snuff out the entire revolt. A Turkish contingent of about twenty thousand troops was able to march on the city of Thebes before heading across the Isthmus to Corinth, easily taking both cities.

But the Turks made a big mistake by crossing through the "narrow defiles" of the Dervenakia, allowing Greek fighters to carry out a wildly successful ambush that left around seventeen thousand of the Turkish soldiers dead. Another Turkish disaster occurred in the city of Missolonghi, where a Turkish contingent, riddled with rampant sickness, was similarly ambushed by Greek guerrilla fighters.

The Turks were decimated, and the commander was so disheartened that he ended his own life. Also in 1822, the Greeks forged their own constitution. The Greek intelligentsia knew full well that in order to have the nations of the world recognize and take their proclaimed independence seriously, they needed the rightful apparatus of an independent state, such as a coherent system of government enshrined in a constitution. Despite this social compact being developed, by 1824, the volunteers were more fractured than ever.

Different rebel leaders seemed to have different aims, and no one could come together well enough to present a unified front against the Ottomans. The Greek revolution then faced a severe challenge in 1825 when armed forces from Egypt were deployed by Ibrahim Pasha, the son of Muhammad Ali, the regional administrator of Egypt. At this time, Egypt was one of the most prosperous and militarily advanced of all of the regions of the Ottoman Empire.

Ibrahim Pasha landed a sizeable force at the harbor of Modon (sometimes known as Methoni) in the western Peloponnese that January. Faced with these odds, the Greeks reached out to the British for aid. The British foreign secretary, George Canning, who was posted in Greece at the time, was handed off the so-called "Act of Submission" by Greek delegates. The document was rather explicit in its aim, stating, "In virtue of the present act, the Greek nation places the sacred deposit of its liberty, independence, and political existence under the absolute protection of Great Britain."

Since the initiative was not in line with Britain's foreign policy at the moment, Canning ultimately declined to pass the missive on. All he could do was advise the Greeks to continue the struggle. One of the primary reasons that the great powers, such as Britain, were hesitant to openly support Greece was that they feared that Russia would become heavily involved, seize territories, and then precipitate a complete collapse of the Ottoman Empire. And the great powers were not yet ready for the massive disruption to the status quo that such an event might bring.

However, by the Spring of 1826, after the fall of the city of Missolonghi, it began to look increasingly likely that the Greek resistance would be snuffed out and that Greece would soon be an Ottoman territory administered by the Egyptians. It was only when the Greeks seemed to be right on the brink of collapse that the foreigners finally came to Greece's aid.

But it must be stressed that in these early days, rather than foreign powers, it was foreign citizens who initially became involved. Due to the great romantic views of Greece among the intellectuals of Europe and America, individual European citizens began to actively support Greece even before their governments sanctioned aid. These zealous volunteers from abroad became collectively known as the "philhellenes," which in Greek basically means one who loves or has a great admiration for Hellenistic culture.

In the Greek War of Independence, droves of volunteer philhellenes came to the lands of Greece to take up the fight for its freedom. But not only did they send people to fight, these philhellenes also raised considerable sums of money to help fund the cost of waging a war against one of the world's most expansive empires. This influx of cold hard cash was especially crucial when it came to healing the fractures of the Greek revolutionaries since much of their infighting could be blamed on a desperation borne of a lack of funds.

With adequate financial assistance, the Greek rebels were able to focus on the real objective—driving out the Turks—rather than squabbling amongst themselves over who was using what resource. The most famous philhellene who arrived on Greece's shores to fight was British poet Lord Byron. Byron was definitely a man in love with Greek culture, and when he heard of Greece's distress, he did not hesitate to lend a hand.

Lord Byron showed up to fight alongside the Greek patriots in January of 1824. Sadly, Byron would perish just a few months later from an illness he had contracted. Even though Byron didn't do much on the actual battlefield, the high-profile nature of his presence alone was a tremendous boost when it came to bringing recognition to the cause. In fact, Byron's death led the public to clamor for a more robust support of Greece.

Soon, the European heads of state—especially Byron's native Britain—were forced to listen. Russia, for its part, was already heading in that direction. The Russian tsar, Alexander I, was initially fearful of what revolutionary chaos might mean for the region, but after hearing of various Turkish massacres and especially the cold-blooded murder of the patriarch of the Greek Orthodox Church, he could no longer ignore what was happening. Russia, after all, viewed itself as the guardian of Orthodox Christianity, and it could not stand by while their Orthodox brothers and sisters were being slaughtered. Another European head of state drawn to the cause was King Charles X of France.

In 1827, these powers came together in London to sign the treaty of the same name—The Treaty of London.

Chapter 12 – The Outside World Gets Involved

"Every man of action has a strong dose of egoism, pride, hardness, and cunning. But all those things will be regarded as high qualities if he can make them the means to achieve great ends."

-Giorgos Seferis

In 1827, Britain, Russia, and France signed an agreement called the Treaty of London in which they recognized the right of Greece to be independent. Furthermore, the treaty stipulated that the Ottoman Empire should recognize Greece's independence as well. The sultan wasn't ready to just lay down after all this fighting, and predictably, he refused to agree to any such terms. It was this refusal that set the stage for the climactic Battle of Navarino.

During this battle, which was waged on October 20th, 1827, the combined might of the European allies decimated a joint Turkish/Egyptian fleet. The Allies located the fleet parked in Navarino Bay. As they approached, the Turks opened fire. Moments later the Allied ships let loose with everything they had. The Turkish craft were stuck in the bay, and they were literally blown out of the water by the heavy artillery fire that was unleashed.

With the destruction of this fleet, Greek independence seemed all but assured. Yet not everyone in the participating Allied countries was all that happy about what had happened. There were some in Britain, for example, who felt that the Allied fleet had overstepped its bounds. In January of 1828, there was a shakeup of the administration, and Britain's Tory Party came to power, charging that England had no business being involved in Greece's struggle. These feelings were later echoed by the king of Great Britain himself when he remarked that the incident was an "untoward event."

Nevertheless, Greece was on the road to statehood, and that January, a man named John Capodistrias (also known as Ioannis Kapodistrias) was poised to become the first head of that newly established state. Capodistrias had been a lifelong bureaucrat, and he was used to some sense of order. Out of a desire to wrest order from what had been a rather chaotic situation, he called for the new constitution to be temporarily suspended so that he could directly control affairs.

Capodistrias was famous for his distrust of Greek's young democracy, stating that the Greeks were not yet ready to make their own decisions. He felt that the most important thing was to have a strong centralized government focused on reversing the damage and decline inflicted on the country by the Ottomans. Capodistrias argued that the Greeks should only focus on democracy when they were on a good enough economic and social footing to do so.

The kind of government that would form in Greece would ultimately be determined by outsiders. Shortly after their intervention at Navarino, Britain, Russia, and France began to debate what should be done with Greece. None of the powers wanted their counterparts to gain a decisive foothold in the region. A British protectorate, a Russian client state, or a French colony would have been anathema to all but the one in control.

So, thankfully for the Greeks, it was rather unanimously agreed that Greece should be an independent state. The great powers, as it turned out, were just as distrustful of Greek democracy as John Capodistrias was, and they began conniving on how to install an authoritarian monarchy in Greece instead. Capodistrias, in the meantime, did not have much longer for this world, as he was assassinated by his rivals on October 9th, 1831.

In the following year, 1832, the European allies finally installed their handpicked monarch on the Greek throne. Seventeen-year-old Otto (the son of King Ludwig I of Bavaria) became the first king of the independent Kingdom of Greece. However, the kingdom that Otto was to rule over was essentially bankrupt. Things were so bad, in fact, that roving bands of Greeks could be found foraging in the wilderness just to keep from starving to death.

Otto was faced with a devastated economy and social unrest, and the situation only continued to deteriorate until massive protests, which were ultimately embraced by large factions of the Greek military, broke out in 1843. These protests pressured the king to forge a new constitution and to create a "two chamber parliament," which consisted of the *Gerousia* (the senate) and the *Vouli* (the lower house of representatives).

National elections would now be held, although rampant corruption in office positions and fraud at the ballot box would become commonplace. In what was perhaps one of the greatest ironies of Greek history, the conditions of the free and independent Greece had become so unbearable that many began to immigrate to the Greek-speaking communities within the Ottoman Empire!

This was a great embarrassment to Greek revolutionaries, and it helped to give rise to what Greek patriots called the "Megali Idea," which translated basically means, "Big Idea." Greek revolutionaries felt that the smaller rump state of the independent Kingdom of Greece was not big enough and that much more of the former

Greek territories, including the old Byzantine capital of Constantinople, should be restored.

The concept was first introduced in 1844 by Greek Prime Minister John Kolettis (also known as Ioannis Kolettis). Kolettis famously stated, "A Greek is not only a man who lives within this kingdom, but also one who lives in Janina, in Salonika, in Serres, in Adrianople, in Constantinople, in Smyrna, in Trebizond, in Crete, in Samos, and in any land associated with Greek history or the Greek race. There are two main centers of Hellenism: Athens, the capital of the Greek Kingdom and 'the City' [Constantinople], the dream and hope of all Greeks."

These patriotic feelings were also, perhaps surprisingly, encouraged by the reigning monarch, King Otto. At this point in time, Greece was still a constitutional monarchy, with King Otto at its head. However, Otto's reign would come to an end in 1862 when revolutionaries took to the streets and demanded a new constitution be forged for Greek society. The outside powers would then appoint George I of Denmark as the new monarch, and a new constitution and representative government would be formed.

King George I had to contend with a popular movement that craved both domestic reform and expansion abroad. Britain helped satisfy some of these cravings by handing over the Ionian Islands to the Greek mainland shortly after George was placed on the throne. With the desire for territorial expansion satiated, King George focused on constitutional reforms, which were completed in 1864. The Senate, which was considered unrepresentative, was tossed out in favor of a more representative single legislative body.

This move gave more direct democracy to the Greek population, but the king still had veto power, as he was able to select and reject ministers at will and even dissolve whole legislative bodies outright. But despite these changes, corruption and voter fraud, especially around election time, remained high. Nevertheless, the bright spot in all of this was the fact that the Greek economy began to improve.

And by the late 1800s, Greece had developed a distinct middle class.

International intrigue was afoot once again in 1866 when the former Greek island of Crete rose up against the Ottoman Empire. In this struggle, the Crete revolutionaries looked toward their fellow Greeks of the mainland for help. Individual Greeks answered the call, and like the philhellenes who were present during the Greek War of Independence, these Greeks managed to add to the military might of those on the ground, as well as raise money for them from abroad.

The great European powers, however, did not want to upset the balance of power by giving too much to the Greeks and disrupting the Ottomans. As such, the Greek government was informed in no uncertain terms that the Greeks would be punished if they did not cease and desist all aid to Crete. This was an embarrassing development for revolutionary-minded Greeks, and it served to remind them that they were still being forced to do the bidding of foreign powers.

In the meantime, the Ottoman Empire began to shift its strategy against the Greeks by seeking to inflame tensions between the Greeks and their Bulgarian neighbors in the Balkans. One of the masterstrokes of this strategy emerged in 1870 when the Ottoman sultan approved the creation of an independent church for the Bulgarians, one that was separate from the main Greek Orthodox Church of Constantinople. The Bulgarians no longer had to look toward the Greeks; they could now dictate the tenants of their faith on their own.

Many Greeks saw this as nothing short of a "divide and conquer" technique. These developments were followed by the so-called Great Eastern Crisis, which rocked Greece and its neighbors in 1875. The crisis began when Montenegro and Serbia launched an assault on Ottoman holdings in Anatolia. The situation then really came to a head when the Russians decided to aid the insurgents. This led to the Russo-Turkish War of 1877.

During the course of the conflict, the Russian forces drove deep into Ottoman territory and parked just outside of Constantinople. Many people back in Greece thought that perhaps this was the moment that would finally fulfill their "Megali Idea" and that the old Byzantine capital of Constantinople would soon be restored. But these hopes were dashed when the parties involved in the war signed the San Stefano Treaty.

Instead of the treaty enabling a larger Greece, it actually created a larger Bulgaria. It seems that Russia was more interested in what was termed "Pan-Slavism" than it was Pan-Hellenism, as it helped its Slavic counterparts expand their base. However, the other European powers did not agree with Russia's aims, and a hastily convened congress was formed, which came up with an international settlement. The larger Bulgaria plan was then scrapped.

Still, a resurgent Bulgaria would become an increasingly competitive element for Greece to take into consideration. Greece would make some gains soon enough, though. In 1881, the British had the Ottomans hand over Arta and Thessaly to Greece. However, these gains were seriously threatened in 1897, with the next round of fighting between the Turks and Greeks.

This latest conflict totally backfired on the Greeks, as the Turks gained the upper hand and came close to taking Athens. Before the Greeks were delivered a knockout blow, the great powers intervened and put an end to the fighting. Although this saved Greece from complete destruction, it was a humiliating defeat, and Greece had to agree to relinquish its recent gains, as well as pay the sultan a fixed indemnity. This setback would put the Megali Idea on hold until the First World War broke out.

Chapter 13 – Greece during the First World War

"When General Allenby conquered Jerusalem during World War I, he was hailed in the American press as Richard the Lion-Hearted, who had at last won the Crusades and driven the pagans out of the Holy Land."

-Noam Chomsky

At the dawn of the 20th century, the Ottoman Empire was tottering at the edge of collapse. Sick of foreign interference, a group called the Young Turks came to prominence, seeking to correct the course of the failing empire. The Young Turks were more nationalists than imperialists, and they left many of the non-Turkish members of the empire wondering what their ultimate fate would be.

Also alarming to some was the fact that the Young Turk movement was closely aligning itself with the rising European power of Germany. The Balkans, too, were a source of great turmoil at this time, and after Austria made the decision to incorporate Bosnia and Hercegovina into its empire, the stage was already being set for World War One.

Back in Greece, dissatisfaction with the status quo had once again reached a fever pitch. In 1910, the newly elected prime minister, Eleutherios Venizelos, led this charge. He was a populist leader, who, among other things, championed the idea of reclaiming the Greek island of Crete from the Ottomans, and his support was only increased when his Liberal Party won the majority of seats in the Greek Parliament in 1912. Venizelos was a charismatic politician, and he was able to shore up support from an important figure on the international stage—British chancellor of the exchequer, David Lloyd George.

At this time, the British were increasingly suspicious of the Ottoman Empire due to its increasing coziness with the Germans. Venizelos was able to use this distrust in order to gain more leverage for the Greek cause. With the British in his back pocket, Prime Minister Venizelos began a dialogue with Greece's Balkan neighbors and established what was known as the Balkan League, which was basically a "defensive" pact between Greece, Bulgaria, Serbia, and Montenegro.

Then, the Montenegrins began the onslaught by waylaying a Turkish troop detachment in Albania. A little over a week later, the Greeks, along with the Bulgarians and Serbs, joined the fray. The Turks stationed in Albania were overwhelmed, and they were pushed back to Turkey. After this occurred, the Greek navy then went to action, blocking the sea lanes. With the sea lanes under the control of Greek naval craft, the Bulgarian troops marched on Turkey.

By November 8th, 1912, the Greeks had poured into Thessalonica, retaking the city for Greece for the first time since the Ottomans had seized it in 1430 CE. But this was all just a prelude to what was to come. Soon after this, a Serb from the Balkans would assassinate the archduke of Austria, Franz Ferdinand, and the whole world would erupt into war as a result.

A year prior to the archduke's assassination, King George I of Greece had been killed while on a sightseeing tour of Thessalonica. King George, who had ruled for nearly fifty years, was already making plans for his son and heir, Constantine, to succeed him. So, as traumatic as his assassination was, the monarchy was already primed for his replacement.

The fact that the new king was named Constantine and that the Greeks felt they were on the verge of claiming Roman Emperor Constantine's old city of Constantinople was certainly not lost on the imagination of the Greek public. It now seemed like the Megali Idea could really happen.

It was while all of these stirring notions were afoot in Greece that the First World War erupted. After Archduke Franz Ferdinand of Austria was killed, Austria demanded that Serbia do something about it. However, the demands were too draconian for Serbia's tastes, and the Serbs refused to acquiesce to all of the listed demands. This led to Austria declaring war on Serbia on July 25th, 1914. As soon as Austro-Hungarian troops appeared on the Serbian border, the Serbs naturally looked toward Russia for help. And as Russian troops mobilized and prepared to intervene, Austria's German allies mobilized as well.

The Germans called for the Russians to back off, but the Russians absolutely refused to do so. This led to Germany declaring war on Russia. The Ottoman Empire, eager to both get revenge on Russia for past wars and to further cultivate its growing relationship with Germany, immediately sided with the Germans and declared war on Russia. Shortly thereafter, Britain and France declared war on Germany.

World War One is generally known as a war fought between the Allied Powers of Britain, France, Russia, (and later the United States) and the Central Powers of Germany, Austria-Hungary, and the Ottoman Empire. But such categorization is confusing and largely inadequate in a variety of ways. For one thing, the Ottoman

Empire wasn't exactly a "central power" as much as an eastern one. The role of Greece, too, would have been ill defined. After all, Greece could be called a "central power," yet Greece most certainly would not have sided with the Central Powers that were active during World War One. Nevertheless, for the sake of clarity and continuity, for this section, we will go ahead and refer to Britain and its allies as the Allied Powers, and we will refer to Germany and its allies as the Central Powers.

Greece saw the war as a golden opportunity to pick apart the bones of the dying Ottoman Empire, so Greece naturally sided with the Allied Powers of Russia, Britain, and France. Venizelos, in particular, was convinced that British naval supremacy would allow for an easy win. And so, hedging his bets with Britain and its allies, Prime Minister Venizelos calculated that once the war concluded, Greece would be in a good place to ride the Allies' coattails all the way to Constantinople.

Venizelos's aspirations were greatly bolstered in January of 1915 when his British handlers informed him that there was talk of important concessions on the coast of Asia Minor (Turkey) that would be given to Greece should the Ottoman Empire be defeated. Venizelos, in turn, suggested that Greece might be able to part with some territory in Macedonia if it was allowed greater gains in Asia Minor. This disturbed some of Venizelos's opponents, and it even provoked a rift between the prime minister and the king, who felt that Venizelos was giving up too much, too soon, in return for Britain's empty promises.

This rift led to Venizelos resigning from his post. The king then went against the wishes of the public by appointing a new prime minister, one Dimitrios Gounaris. Thinking the war to be a folly, the king and his court then went against the popular sentiment of the times and did everything in their power to keep Greece out of the fight. This provoked the anger of the British and the French, who were counting on Greece to come into the war as their ally.

Nevertheless, Britain invoked its guardian status over Greece as outlined in the Treaty of Protection of 1853 and began to station troops in Greek territory. If the Greek people weren't going to fight, the British figured they would at least use Greek land as bases of operation for their own forces.

Greece, in the meantime, was in the midst of incredible turmoil. The majority of the Greek people wanted to join the fight against the Central Powers, but the king of Greece was just as determined to keep Greece out. It is rather rare when a whole nation seems clamoring to fight and a cautious leader is trying their best to keep them from doing so. Most of the time it is the other way around. Just think of the Vietnam War in which you had a string of United States presidents escalating the conflict while the public protested US involvement.

The politically exiled populist leader Venizelos set up what could be termed as a virtual opposition government within Greece, which became the center for his base of supporters. However, the greatest pressure on the king came from Britain and France. Infuriated at Greece's refusal to take part, these two European powers began to strip Greece's national government of any agency of its own. Part of the draconian measures included the immediate expulsion of anyone found to be a so-called "enemy agent." This meant that any Greek suspected of collaborating with or spying for the Central Powers could be immediately kicked out of the country.

Even more embarrassing than this overreach were demands for the Greek military to disarm. Naval ships were supposed to remove their guns, and even shore batteries had to be taken down. The king could not sit back and allow his country to be so thoroughly emasculated like this. King Constantine obstinately refused to meet any of these demands.

After his refusal, the Allies came down hard on Greece and demanded that the king step down from power. French and British soldiers came ashore near Athens at the port city of Piraeus, and a naval blockade was enacted over all of southern Greece in order to pressure the king to stand down. By January of 1917, the king had had enough, and he announced that he was going to resign in favor of allowing his son Alexander to become king in his place. As soon as King Constantine was gone and the new king was installed, the opposition party of Venizelos was put back into power.

Greece now had both the public will and the political apparatus to head into the war full force on the side of the Allies. However, things did not go well for Greece at the outset, with the Greek army taking a high number of casualties when they first entered the fray in the spring of 1917. A battlefield success was not achieved until the following year when, in May of 1918, victories were scored against Bulgaria in the Balkans. This again brought forth hope that perhaps Greece could ride the tide of the Allied Powers' success when the war ultimately concluded.

Greece faced another major offensive against the Bulgarians on September 14th, 1918, in which a joint force of Greek and British soldiers stormed into the Vardar Valley of Macedonia and engaged Bulgarian troops stationed around Lake Dorian. The battle was largely a stalemate, but after a prolonged onslaught, the Bulgarians were finally forced to retreat. With the Bulgarians on the run, the Allies shifted strategies and decided to mobilize British and Greek forces to the eastern Ottoman front.

At this point in the war, the situation had changed dramatically. Even though the Allies were gaining ground, they had been hit with the setback of Russia being knocked out of the war. Russia had been beset with internal turmoil from the beginning, and it suffered through a communist revolution in 1917 that overthrew the Russian tsar while Russian troops were still in the trenches. The new Russian/Soviet leadership then quickly moved to end Russia's involvement with the war.

This was a great victory for the Central Powers, but even so, the Ottoman Empire, for one, seemed to be on its last legs. The Ottomans put up a ferocious fight in the beginning phases of the war, but they were now running out of fuel. Greek advocates of the Megali Idea believed that the time to retake Constantinople from Turkey had arrived. But before the Greek army could advance farther, news was received that the worn-down Ottomans had already agreed to sign an armistice.

Once again, the Greeks were thwarted right at the gates of Constantinople, and they were forced to stand down. It was now understood that any further territorial gains for Greece would have to be hammered out through diplomatic negotiations rather than on the battlefield. Nevertheless, it was a great political victory for Greek Prime Minister Venizelos since his belief in the triumph of the Allied Powers had been fulfilled.

Greece also managed to arrive at the scene of this victory in very good shape. Since Greece had entered the war so late, unlike the other Allies, it had been largely shielded from heavy casualties, yet it was still able to claim a seat at the victor's table. In order to reconcile with his most vehement detractors in Greece, Venizelos needed to make sure that Greece was rewarded handsomely for its efforts. Knowing that his skills would be needed to pressure and cajole the Allies to give him the favorable terms he needed, Venizelos embarked on a grand tour of Europe to discuss Greece's post-war plans.

All of this finagling behind the scenes was done in the lead-up to the Paris Peace Conference, which was held in January of 1919. During this conference, the post-war order would be discussed. Venizelos believed that his aims for Greece would be achieved after meeting with the Allied nations to show them his way of thinking. Venizelos spoke before the Council of Ten (the heads of government of the major parties involved in the war) in February of 1919 and laid out his territorial claims.

Right in line with the Megali Idea, Venizelos's demands were indeed big—he insisted on Greek control of Epirus, Thrace, and the Turkish islands of the Aegean, as well as certain islands of the Dodecanese that had been previously claimed by Italy. But even more pressing, he insisted on regaining much of western Turkey where large Greek settlements existed. And although he stopped just short of demanding the return of Constantinople to Greek control, he suggested that Constantinople might become an "international" city. Most of the people present at the conference understood that the internationalization of Constantinople would simply be one further step toward Greece eventually claiming the city as its own.

As provocative as Venizelos's demands were, the Ottoman Empire was in no position to argue. With the whole regime on life support, it was all they could do to keep from completely collapsing. It was actually the Italians who caused the most trouble for these Greek demands since Italy had no intention of giving up any of the islands of the Dodecanese. The Italians were also insulted at the notion that they should concede anything in light of the fact that they had fought harder and longer than the Greeks during the war. The Italians expected to be rewarded with new territory rather than having to give anything up to anyone. In fact, the Italians were so incensed by these demands that Italian warships were sent off the coast of Smyrna in western Turkey in order to intimidate the Greeks.

This led Venizelos to request permission to land troops of his own to protect the territory, which he hoped would soon become part of Greece. He was granted this allowance, and in May of 1919, Greek soldiers arrived on Anatolian shores to prevent any unilateral action on the part of the Italians. This action was enough to deter the Italians, and Smyrna began to function as an unofficial part of the Greek state.

Matters were then made official on August 10th, 1920, when the Turkish government entered into the Treaty of Sèvres. This treaty granted Greece Smyrna, as well as a big chunk of the surrounding territory of western Anatolia. The Greeks were also granted the Sea of Marmara's northern coast, in addition to control of the Gallipoli Peninsula, Thrace, and the Aegean Islands.

The Megali Idea seemed to be alive and well, but like the best ideas of mice and men, it would not take much for this victory to come undone.

Chapter 14 – Greece in between World Wars

"Greece expects you not merely to die for her, for that is little, indeed; she expects you to conquer. That is why each of you, even in dying, should be possessed by one thought alone—how to conserve your strength to the last so that those who survive may conquer. And you will conquer, I am sure of this."

-Eleutherios Venizelos

The arrival of Greek troops in Asia Minor set off a cascade of resentment and fury within the Turkish populations of Asia Minor. Although the government of the Ottoman Empire had been defeated, many in the public did not wish to give up the fight for what they considered vital pieces of their homeland. A Turk by the name of Mustafa Kemal (also known as Kemal Ataturk) took up the banner of resistance and demanded that a new nationalistic Turkish government be formed to prevent the foreign encroachments that the defeated Ottoman state seemed incapable of fending off.

In the fall of 1919, Kemal, riding on a tide of popular Turkish sentiment, had already entered into a dialogue with the Allied Powers, insisting that the sultan had so disgraced himself that he no longer represented the true intentions of the Turks. The Allied

Powers knew that this bold man's movement within the Ottoman Empire was indeed a strong one, and the tottering Ottoman government seemed entirely unable to rein it in.

This was of grave concern, as it meant that whatever agreements were reached with the Ottoman government would be rendered null and void if an internal revolution occurred and the Ottoman Empire collapsed outright. These fears seemed to come to fruition in 1920 when the Turkish parliament prepared to declare the emergence of a Turkish national state from the ruins of the Ottoman Empire.

Suddenly, there were two governments in the Turkish domain—the sultan's in Constantinople (Istanbul) and Mustafa Kamal's own seat of power in Ankara, Turkey. Riding on a wave of popular support, Kamal rejected the punishing Treaty of Sèvres entirely and made it known that he would not consider abiding by it for one second.

To the chagrin of the Greeks, the European powers seemed to lose the will to fight and instead began to enter into discussions with the Turkish nationalists. In a last-ditch effort for support, Venizelos reached out to his old British friend, David Lloyd George, to see if he could secure a pledge of British support for military action against the Turkish nationalists, but his requests were not indulged. Britain and the other Allied Powers were now ready to move on. Greece would be on its own.

Along with the threat of the mobilization of Turkish nationalists, Greece began to suffer from its own internal turmoil. First, King Alexander unexpectedly passed away, and in a decidedly bizarre manner. As ridiculous as it sounds, the young king was bitten by a monkey and died from an infection that resulted from the bite. It sounds like something straight out of a tabloid newspaper: "Greek King Bit by Monkey—Dies Terrible Death." But it is the truth.

Apparently, King Alexander was an animal lover, and he had his own personal zoo on the palace grounds. One of his monkeys had gotten into an altercation with his dog, and King Alexander tried to separate them. It was at this point that another monkey nearby jumped on the king and bit him. This bite led to Alexander perishing from blood poisoning on October 25th, 1920. This shock was then coupled with the even greater seismic shift of Venizelos and his party being voted out of power in the November 1920 election.

The party voted in supported bringing back the previous non-expansionist king—Constantine. They successfully voted for this action to be taken, and Constantine was back on the throne that December. Even if the public was still strongly supportive of the Megali Idea, the Greek political landscape was now unstable. And after Venizelos's party was booted out, the new political power players began to remove officials who had previously been loyal to Venizelos. Venizelos himself was deeply dismayed by this chaos, and in a state of depressed resignation, he left Greece entirely to live in what amounted to a self-imposed exile abroad.

Greece had a falling out with the European powers, which remained entirely disenchanted with King Constantine. Britain's most famous statesmen, Winston Churchill, had an interesting take on the whole matter. In light of the communist takeover of Russia, Churchill argued that the Turkish nationalists were the best bulwark against communism in the region. He further insisted that Greek control of the region would be weak and inconsistent, making Turkey vulnerable to communist insurgencies.

The Greeks now saw the writing on the wall, and they knew that their international partners were bailing on them. The Greek supporters of the Megali Idea felt that a repeat of Smyrna was in order. It had taken a show of military force to convince the world that Smyrna belonged to Greece, and if further acquisitions were to be had, it would take another strong showing.

It was with this strategy in mind that the Greek army launched a surprise attack on the capital of the Turkish nationalists, Ankara, on March 23rd, 1921. The attack did not go well, and at least part of the reason why can be attributed to the fact that King Constantine had purged the military of officers who had previously supported Venizelos.

The results of this fateful decision would become quite clear on the battlefield. At one point during the course of the conflict, a group of some 200,000 Greeks were repulsed by the Turkish troops. As the Greeks retreated, they left some twenty thousand dead Greek soldiers behind. The Greeks had found themselves in a very dangerous situation in Anatolia. Along with having to face the resurgent forces of the Turkish nationalists, the Greeks also had to deal with a largely hostile Turkish population who had found itself under Greek control.

Yes, even though the Greek residents of western Anatolia may have been happy with being annexed to Greece, the Turkish residents, who made up a significant number of the population, were not too pleased with the notion. In their eyes, the Greeks were not liberators but a hostile occupying force. As such, the Greek forces could expect nothing but antagonism and even outright attacks from the Turkish locals.

So, even if the Turkish national troops were kept at bay, it would be extremely challenging for the Greeks to administer a region in which a large segment of the population was vehemently against the Greek presence. Even more troubling was the prospect of what might happen to the native Greek residents if the Greek army was to leave western Anatolia. As had been the case for hundreds of years, the Greeks of western Anatolia were in danger of reprisals and even outright massacres at the hands of the Turks. If the Greek military was to suddenly leave, all of the anger and hostility toward the Greek occupation would undoubtedly be targeted at the remaining Greek civilian population. It is possible that a collective

pogrom would have been carried out against them by the vengeful Turks.

Due to these fears, it was later determined by the cooler heads that prevailed at the bargaining table that a population exchange program would be the only means to stave off such bloody reprisals. This was a drastic measure for sure, but it would later prove to be the only means to prevent outright genocide from occurring against the Greeks who would ultimately be left behind.

At any rate, the moment of truth came on August 26th, 1922, when the Turks launched a massive offensive that sent the Greek troops in full retreat toward the western Anatolian coastlines. By early September, Greek forces were evacuating from the region. With the Greek troops gone, Turkish troops took control of Smyrna on September 11th, 1922. Almost immediately thereafter, a terrible massacre commenced in which scores of Greek residents were killed. This was followed a couple of days later by a large fire that ended up burning much of the town to the ground.

Coincidentally enough (or perhaps on purpose), the only section of Smyrna that survived the destruction was the Turkish quarter. It is estimated that about 25,000 people died in the inferno, and another 200,000 were left without any resources of which to speak. Many of those left destitute in the rubble actually made their way to the coast, desperately hoping for aid from mainland Greece. Greece, in the meantime, was forced to come to terms, and it hammered out a truce called the Treaty of Lausanne.

Although Greece was soundly defeated by the Turks, the terms were still fairly favorable to the Greeks. While they had to give up any claims to land in Anatolia, they were allowed to keep most of the territory it had prior to World War One. The most lasting impact of the treaty, however, was the aforementioned "population exchange" with the Turks, which was set into motion in May of 1923. The idea of exchanging entire populations based upon ethnicity is certainly controversial, but in light of the smoking ruins of Smyrna and the threat of subsequent massacres, it was viewed as the only way to prevent further reprisals against minority populations.

So, the Greek populations of Anatolia were exchanged for the Turkish populations of Greece. The only Greeks to remain were the 100,000 or so in Constantinople who had a guarantee of international protection, which allowed them to stay in the only home they had ever known. Greece greatly benefited from the importation of a highly skilled labor pool of Ottoman Greeks. Many of the new arrivals had been quite prosperous in the Ottoman Empire and began to lend their skills to Greece itself.

One major development was the introduction of Greek/Turkish-styled tobacco farming. Tobacco soon became the number one trading commodity for Greece as a result. But in the immediate aftermath of the war, few could see the positives that would later develop. At the time, it was a dark period of animosity and recriminations.

In the aftermath of the Smyrna disaster, the Greek king had dismissed parliament and formed a new party led by one Triandafillakos. This move was not popular with the general public or the Greek armed forces, the latter of which, led by Colonel Stylianos Gonatas, decided to let their voices be heard by dropping leaflets all over Athens by air on September 26th, explicitly calling for King Constantine to step down. Knowing that his time was up, King Constantine obliged, and he resigned as king the following day. Shortly thereafter, a provisional government was established in Athens by Greek General Theodoros Pangalos, along with his colleagues and fellow generals, Gargalidis and Mazaakis. With the support of some twelve thousand troops at their disposal.

Power was then given to a revolutionary committee, which had to sort out the state's affairs. King Constantine and his family were shipped off to their exile in Palermo. King George II was installed in his place. King George II's reign was rather short-lived, though;

in April of 1924, the Greek public cast their votes at the ballot box in favor of the creation of the Hellenic Republic. It is said that 758,472 Greeks voted in favor of forming the Hellenic republic, while 325,322, voted to keep the constitutional monarchy.

Among those who voted for the republic was a considerable portion of recent Greek refugees. The Greek refugees associated the idea of a king with the failures of the Greco-Turkish War that had uprooted them from their homes. So, it is really no wonder they would have voted to abolish the monarchy.

The refugees also tended to be supporters of Venizelists. However, in June of 1925, a military takeover was orchestrated by General Theodoros Pangalos. This military government was, in turn, toppled by yet another coup, which was launched in the summer of 1926 by Colonel Georgios Kondylis. The only hope for the Greeks appeared to be the ballot box, and droves went to vote in 1928. After the 1928 election, Venizelos and his party were voted back into power.

Venizelos's first effort in office was to create strong relations with Greece's neighbors. He signed agreements with Italy and Yugoslavia, and he opened up dialogue with Albania. But perhaps most importantly, he sought to tamp down the discontent of the public by improving Greece's economy. He did this by focusing on improving agricultural production, as well as improving the nation's infrastructure. He also made sure that the school systems were modernized and made available to the populace.

Initially, the reforms went over well, for the Greeks now had enough food to eat, decent roads on which to drive, and good schools to which to send their kids. This was definitely an improvement, but these improvements were sharply curtailed in 1929 with the start of the worldwide economic downturn known as the Great Depression. The Great Depression affected many nations around the globe, but interestingly enough, one of the most negative impacts was the fact that Greeks in the United States found themselves unemployed and were therefore unable to send money back home to Greece. A large part of the Greek economy had been aided by these remittance payments, which collectively stimulated the Greek financial markets.

In many countries around the world, failed economies had become the playground of communist uprisings. Communists often used an economic collapse as a reason to point to the perceived failures of capitalism and to call for the centralized control of world economies by communist states. Fearing the same forces might try to take advantage of the economic troubles in Greece, Venizelos tried to head communism off at the pass by issuing the so-called "Idionymon Law," which made it illegal to have political association with groups that tried to undermine the social order. This meant, of course, that the communist party, which called for the overthrow of capitalism, would be entirely banned from Greece.

As fate would have it, Venizelos was voted out of office in 1933. Due to his electoral defeat, it seemed that his policies might be dead in the water. However, shortly after his defeat, Venizelos's supporters in the military attempted to launch a coup. The coup failed, and in the backlash against Venizelos and all who supported him, an attempt was made on Venizelos's life. Thankfully for Venizelos, this attempt failed just as the coup had, and in one of the most dramatic moments in Greek history, Venizelos was seen stepping out of a car filled with bullet holes, unharmed. This event seemed to set a fire in Venizelos's soul, and he tried one last uprising himself. In the spring of 1935, he staged a revolt against the government.

However, it did not go quite so well, and Venizelos was ultimately forced to flee to Rhodes. He would die roughly one year later in March of 1936 as an exile in Paris, France. This marked the end of the Venizelos movement. Not only was their leader dead, but those who had supported or even just sympathized with him were also steadily removed from any and all positions of power.

Those who wished to restore the monarchy were now in a powerful position, and in November of 1935, they did just that, installing King George II back on the throne.

King George II then selected a Greek army officer—Ioannis Metaxas—as the next prime minister on April 13th, 1936. Metaxas was authoritarian in the extreme, and in what must have been one of the most comical sessions of parliament ever, he bullied parliamentarians to vote themselves out of existence, with 241 members voting for the suspension of parliament.

The only real resistance to Metaxas was the remaining communist element. This group managed to put together several labor strikes in May of 1936, the climax of which was a massive strike that hit the tobacco industry in Thessalonica. These efforts produced such a backlash that these subversive actors were completely shut down, as Metaxas convinced the king to censor the news media and curtail other constitutional rights. Soon, workers were no longer allowed to gather for strikes at all.

Metaxas was now the real power behind the throne, and he began to mobilize 1930s Greece into what could only be described as an authoritarian, fascist state. But although Greece was taking on the trappings of a fascist dictatorship, it would not fall in line with similar movements that were afoot in Spain, Italy, and Germany. Greek fascism would remain peculiarly isolated and even at odds with its similarly fascist counterparts. Part of the reason for this was the simple fact that Greece was still greatly beholden to Great Britain. Greece could not risk getting out of Britain's good graces, and unless Britain itself were to suddenly turn fascist, there was no way that Greece would risk its relationship with Britain by getting cozy with Italy, Spain, or Germany.

So, ideology aside, when World War Two commenced in 1939, Greece chose a course of pragmatism and did everything it could to stay out of the growing conflict. Greece's Mediterranean neighbor Italy would decide to push the issue. Italy invaded Albania in April of 1939, placing Italian troop detachments right across the Greek border. Fascist Italian dictator Benito Mussolini then delivered an ultimatum to Metaxas on October 28th, 1940, demanding that he allow Italian troops to move across the border to occupy certain strategic positions. And these demands had to be met in the next few hours.

It is said that when Metaxas was alerted to these impetuous demands, he declared, "I could not make a decision to sell my house on a few hours' notice. How do you expect me to sell my country? No!" As controversial as he was, Metaxas's "No!" would become Greece's rallying cry during the course of the conflict. Mussolini almost certainly knew that his demands would be rejected, and before the arbitrary deadline set for compliance had even run out, Italian troops were crossing over into Greece.

But even though Mussolini thought he was going to bully the Greeks into submission, he was in for a big surprise. Because as divided and chaotic as Greece had become over the last few years, the invasion of the Italians served to unite the Greeks together against a common enemy. And just about everyone was suddenly taking up Metaxas's rallying cry of "No!" The Greek forces quickly mobilized and managed to completely encircle the invading 3rd Alpine Division of Italy.

With this group of Italian troops neutralized, the Greek troops quickly turned the tables on the Italians and rapidly marched north to invade Italian-controlled Albania. This reversal was a severe embarrassment to Italy's ambition, but it did not necessarily mean that Greece would be pushed out of its position of neutrality. It was actually the British who would pull the Greeks into a war with Germany by insisting that the Greeks join them as an official ally in the struggle.

Britain began to suggest that the Greeks should allow British troops to be deployed in Greece. Knowing this would bring the full fury of Germany down on Greece, Metaxas refused to allow the

British to do so. Metaxas soon would not have a say in the matter, though. On January 29th, 1941, he unexpectedly died of what has been described as a bad case of "phlegmon of the pharynx." He was then succeeded by Alexandros Koryzis.

Koryzis decided to take the British up on their offer, and he agreed to allow the British Expeditionary Force to land on Greek soil. The British arrived in March of 1941, and shortly thereafter, Adolf Hitler made the fateful decision to invade Greece. The reasoning behind this invasion was that he had already been planning a sneak attack on the Soviet Union, and having Allied forces to the south of German troops marching through the Balkans was viewed as an intolerable position in which to be.

So, predictably enough (and just as Metaxas feared would be the case), the Germans launched an invasion of Greece to clear out the Allies. If the British and Greeks had more time to solidify their positions, it is possible they could have repulsed the Germans, but as it was, the joint British-Greek forces had been hastily prepared and were not ready for the massive onslaught Nazi Germany was about to unleash upon them.

Chapter 15 – Greece during the Second World War

"Fascism, the more it considers and observes the future and the development of humanity, quite apart from political considerations of the moment, believes neither in the possibility nor the utility of perpetual peace."

-Benito Mussolini

Greece managed to stay out of World War Two for the first couple years of the fight, but in 1941, after Prime Minister Metaxas perished, his successor, Alexandros Koryzis, allowed the British to land troops on Greek soil, therefore ending Greek neutrality. Once Greece was officially in the Allies' orbit, Germany did not hesitate to invade. In April of 1941, the Germans, with some Italian auxiliaries, launched an invasion into the Greek heartland.

There was confusion from the start since the Greeks and the British had different strategies for the defense of Greece. The British wished for the Greeks to pull back so they could mobilize in the more defensible terrain of the Aliakmon Line. The Greeks, however, refused to give an inch of their territory to the invaders and stayed where they were. Thus, when the German army entered Greece, it found disorder and a lack of coordination in the ranks.

The Germans split into three main groups. One group drove south, pinning the Greek forces there, and the other two drove east to slam into Greek defenders in Thessaloniki. German forces managed to reach Athens on April 18th. As the Germans poured in, Greek Prime Minister Alexandros Koryzis made the fateful decision to take his own life. Martial law had been declared in the city, and the general public was informed that Koryzis had died of a heart attack rather than by suicide so as not to inflame tensions in the city even further. Greek politician Emmanouil Tsouderos would be appointed to succeed him.

The masterstroke came when the Germans cut off the British army, isolating them from the Greek forces. By the end of the month, British forces were retreating toward Corinth. The Germans would once again cut them off by deploying paratroopers onto the Isthmus of Corinth on April 26th, blocking their exit.

Despite the odds being stacked against their escape, the British and their commonwealth allies—some fifty thousand in all—managed to march north once again and make their way through the mountains of Roumeli They then made their way to the shores of the Peloponnese, where they were evacuated and taken to the island of Crete, which was still under Allied control.

The key word here is "still" since it would not be under Allied control for much longer. In the following month, on May 20th, the Germans launched an all-out assault on Crete. The Germans employed some four hundred bombers and dive bombers to blast the British positions to smithereens and then again used paratroopers and even their glider troops (German soldiers on hang gliders) to swarm the island. As daring as the German paratroopers and glider troopers were, some found themselves on a suicide mission because as much as German airpower had attempted to pound Allied defenses into submission, the defenders were still able to take pot shots at the Germans whenever they had a chance.

Others got caught on trees and other terrain and were massacred by angry villagers. But despite these losses, the Germans proved to be unstoppable. They had complete control of the skies and the surrounding area; it was only a matter of time before Crete fell. Before all was lost, the British did manage to evacuate King George and then Prime Minister Emmanouil Tsouderos, but Greek freedom itself was temporarily snuffed out. Once the Greeks were defeated by the Axis, Greek territory was divvied up between German, Bulgarian, and Italian zones.

This was certainly not what Italian dictator Mussolini had intended since he wanted to conquer all of Greece and incorporate it into his fascist Italian empire. But due to all of his previous blunders and inept abilities as a military commander, this was the arrangement for which he had to settle.

The Italian occupation zone was in western Greece, and it has been said that the Italian occupation was a fairly benign one. But the Greeks were still cognizant of the fact that it was the Italians who had started this whole mess, so they were most certainly not in the mood to make nice with the Italians. The German occupation zone, predictably enough, was the most brutal and oppressive.

It did not take much for the Greeks to end up on the wrong side of the Germans. They ran their sector as a totalitarian police state, and one wrong move could get a Greek resident hauled off to be imprisoned, tortured, or killed. In May of 1941 alone, it is said that two hundred villagers in the German-controlled village of Kastelli were shot and killed due to alleged insubordination. In 1943, an even worse incidence of mass murder occurred when 1,400 were killed in the town of Kalavryta.

Having said that, if the Germans were trying to win the hearts and minds of those they occupied, they sure had a funny way of showing it. And of course, for the Jewish residents, the consequences of German occupation were even more terrible. It is said that in Thessalonica alone, which had a Jewish community that dated back several centuries, over fifty thousand Jews were gathered up and sent to concentration camps. Due to the systematic removal conducted by the Germans, by 1942, the old Jewish quarters of Greece no longer existed.

The rest of the Greeks who remained faced starvation since many of the food imports that made up important staples of their diet were no longer available due to a blockade set up by the Allied Powers. The blockade was put in place to hurt the Axis Powers (Germany, Italy, and Japan), but it actually hurt the Greek civilians trapped under the Axis dominion more. In total, it is said that during the occupation of the Axis, an astonishing 8 percent of the Greek population perished.

Death by malnutrition was a serious threat. According to war historian Mark Mazower, those who were malnourished were easily spotted in the street due to the tumors and boils that would form all over their bodies. This is apparently due to the body's compromised immune system, which had been weakened from a lack of proper food. Bacteria apparently is able to grow unchecked in the pores of the skin when the immune system is significantly weakened from malnutrition. This frightening phenomenon could be seen in the pock-marked faces of many of those starving to death in Nazi-occupied Greece. It also was common for those near death to just suddenly collapse and die.

According to official Ministry of Health Data of in 1942, the rate of deaths in Greece shot up over the rate of births. As anyone can imagine, a society in which people are dying faster than they are being born is most certainly one that is in decline. Another sign was the local cemeteries, which were overwhelmed with a massive influx of dead to bury, especially during the winter months. And for those who did not die, the stress of the ordeal was certainly taking its toll.

The Greek populace was understandably under great strain, and many Greeks were at their wit's end. Many personal accounts have since emerged from survivors. One particularly poignant one comes down to us from a Greek woman by the name of Ionna Tsatsou, who was involved with some homegrown relief efforts at the time. She vividly recalled the desperation of the masses. She herself was more fortunate than most Greeks since she was the wife of an affluent college professor, but she often saw firsthand the havoc that food shortages had on the less fortunate.

She was particularly distressed by the starving children she encountered. The things she saw deeply affected her, and at times, they even haunted her dreams. And on one particular evening, one dream in particular stood out to her. She dreamt of "a large table laid with the most beautiful food and drink. At its head the Christ child was seated, and round him countless little Greek children. All ate compulsively and with gusto, smearing their faces. Among them many of my little friends. I awoke with the feeling of coming out of paradise and sinking slowly but consciously into a familiar nightmare." For her, waking up to the grim reality of Nazi occupation truly was a nightmare of the worst kind.

The Greeks did get some respite in the summer of 1942 when the British relaxed their blockade and allowed wheat to be shipped from Canada to those in need in Greece. This valuable aid was enough to relieve the famine and prevent a multitude of deaths due to starvation. As helpful as all this was, some could not help but blame the British for putting the blockade up in the first place.

But the British, in turn, blamed the occupying Axis Powers for refusing to provide resources to those whom they had conquered. But regardless of how much blame they shared for Greece's burdens, the greatest hope that the Greeks had, at least initially, was that the British would come to their rescue, and there were often rumors of the imminent arrival of a British fleet that would drive the occupiers out.

In the early days of the occupation, the Greeks even showed their defiance by actively fraternizing with British prisoners of war. There were more than a few accounts of Greeks surrounding

German trucks loaded with British prisoners of war and loudly cheering and applauding them. Some were even offered cigarettes and beer. The Germans, of course, were none too pleased, and they would promptly chase the crowds off.

There were also many cases of Greek civilians taking in and sheltering British troops who still remained at large. They did this at great risk to themselves, for if the German authorities learned of what they were doing, they would no doubt be killed. But despite the Greek support of the British, as the days of the occupation wore on, hopes for an early rescue by outside forces increasingly dimmed.

The Greeks were determined to resist their occupiers, though, and it is said that immediately after the regular armies of Greece were defeated, homegrown bands of rebel fighters made their way to the remote mountainous terrain of the nation where they could prepare for the next phase of the war. Known as the "People's War," this phase had regular everyday Greeks prepared to engage in a long, drawn-out spate of guerrilla warfare against their oppressors.

Early on, a leading figure in this struggle for freedom emerged: Athanasios Klaras (also known as Aris Velouchiotis). Klaras was actually an active member of Greek's underground communist party, and he was a known left-wing ideologue. His National Liberation Front, which in Greek was called the Ethniko Apeleftherotiko Metopowhich, or EAM for short, would become the main focal point of resistance against the Axis Powers that occupied Greece.

He was said to have been a charismatic leader, and most importantly as it pertained to the armed resistance, he was a very capable military strategist. Although the roots of the EAM were communist, they were so successful that they ended up attracting Greek people from all ideological backgrounds to their ranks. Not surprisingly, many Greeks were eager to join a common effort to resist the fascist occupation of their country. The group was so successful that in the fall of 1942, the British were able to use them to sabotage an important railway bridge to prevent the Germans from supplying forces farther to the south.

This was of extreme importance, as by this point, the Germans were actively sending supplies down this track of rail to southern Greece and then on to Axis positions in North Africa. The Allies were desperately trying to gain ground in North Africa, and they knew that cutting off this active supply line to the Axis would be of tremendous help. That September, the British actually dropped a small contingent into the mountain stronghold of the guerrilla fighters and helped orchestrate the operation directly from the ground.

Ideologically opposed factions of the resistance were convinced to put aside their differences for the common strategy of defeating the occupiers. The group struck on the evening of November 25th, 1942, successfully disabling the railroad by destroying the Gorgopotamos railway bridge. This was a great boon not only to the resistance but also to the greater war effort since it made Axis positions in North Africa more vulnerable and therefore easier to defeat, as the Allies attempted to use North Africa as a stepping stone to an invasion of Italy.

The Allies were indeed able to leap frog from North Africa to Sicily and then on to Italy. The Italians were unable to face the full force of the Allies, and they quickly came to terms and surrendered on September 8th, 1943. Interestingly enough, at least part of the Allies' success against the Italians was due to an elaborate ruse that had been perpetrated by the British. Known as Operation Mincemeat, the British pulled off a fairly morbid stunt in which they dressed a dead body up as a British officer and left it off the coast of fascist Spain for the Axis to find.

The British planted official looking documents on the corpse that detailed an upcoming Allied attempt to land in Greece and Sardinia. These plans were false, as the Allies were aiming for Sicily and then Italy. The Germans apparently took the bait, and even Hitler was convinced that the invasion would take place in the Greek theater. So, while the Germans were shoring up defenses in Greece, they neglected to fortify their positions around Italy, allowing the Allies to have a much easier time of things than they otherwise would have.

At any rate, as soon as news of Italy's surrender reached Greek ears, many Italian troops were murdered on the spot. The Italian government may have waved the white flag, but even with their hands up, some Greeks were ready for revenge. Although some Greeks sought vengeance on the deposed Italians, there were those who would just as soon celebrate with them. Some disillusioned Italians even began arming the resistance, selling guns, grenades, and other military equipment to the very groups that would continue the struggle against the Germans.

As soon as the Germans got wind of this, it created a predictable firestorm of wrath. The German liaison staff in Athens, General Heinz von Gyldenfeldt, told his Italian counterpart General Carlo Vecchiarelli in no uncertain terms, "If there were a rejection of a continuation of the fight [Italian surrender] then the German Army must, for its own security, be certain that Italian weapons would never be turned on the Germans, i.e., they must be surrendered to the German Army."

The Germans then systematically disarmed the Italians without incident. The German high command then gave the Italian troops the choice of either joining up with German troops or be evacuated from Greece. Most chose the latter. Sadly enough, for the Italians, they were deliberately misled into thinking that they were being evacuated back to Italy. This was not the case, as the Germans likely did not want to repatriate troops that could possibly turn on them later. Instead, they were put on a train that took them straight through the Balkans to Yugoslavia, where they were put in concentration camps and held as prisoners of war.

Not all of the Italians handed over their weapons peacefully. On the island of Rhodes, where the Germans were greatly outnumbered by the Italians, Italian troops refused to comply with German demands. This led to some pretty serious skirmishes between the two until the Germans finally forced the Italians to surrender, resulting in over forty thousand Italian prisoners of war being shipped off by the Germans.

Some Italians in mainland Greece opted for a third option. Rather than joining ranks with the Germans or risk facing deportation, they took to the hills and joined the Greek guerrilla fighters they found there. British intelligence actually estimated that by April of 1944, there were about ten thousand Italians who had joined ranks with the Greeks. At this point, the communist groups were controlling much of the rural countryside, and acting as a state within a state, they were even collecting taxes from the local villagers. It was claimed that these taxes were used to provide for the poor, but many believed it was just to line the pockets of the communists.

With the Italians out of the picture, the Germans redoubled their efforts to put down the Greek rebels, and—if it were even possible—they entered a new level of brutality. None other than German Field Marshal Wilhelm Keitel had advised, "This fight has nothing to do with a soldier's chivalry nor with the decisions of the Geneva Conventions. If this fight against the bands, in the East as well as the Balkans is not carried out with the most brutal means, the forces at our disposal may in the near future not last out to master this plague. The troops are therefore authorized and ordered in this struggle to take any measures without restriction even against women and children if these are necessary for success.

[Humanitarian] considerations of any kind are a crime against the German nation."

This was the backward morality of the Germans during the war. Even while they were committing crimes against humanity, the German high command preached that showing the enemy any sense of compassion or "humanitarian consideration" was in itself considered a crime. Brainwashed with propaganda such as this, German troops acted as exterminators, engaging in the wholesale liquidation of rebels—male, female, young, or old—without any remorse or compassion.

The Italians, for their part, were notorious for fraternizing with the enemy, and many had Greek girlfriends on the side. The Germans, however, were strictly ordered to have no relations with non-Germans. They were simply told to ruthlessly root out and kill their enemies. For the most part, German soldiers seemed to abide by these chilling principles of unrelenting extermination. But no matter how many villages they burned, civilians they massacred, communist strongholds they leveled, the rebellion would not be stamped out.

Roughly a year after the Italians first folded, the German forces were on the run as well. The Soviet push into Romania led the Germans troops to withdraw from Greece in August of 1944 so that they could redeploy to face the more pressing threat of Russian troops storming through eastern Europe. In the meantime, the factions that had been working together in the Greek resistance began to split apart in a full-blown civil war, as communist forces and more conservative forces began to battle for the future of the post-war Greek state.

That October, even as British troops were landing on Greek shores, the communist Greek People's Liberation Army managed to gain the upper hand when they took over the Greek capital of Athens. Before World War Two was over, one of the major flashpoints of what would become the Cold War had already begun.

Chapter 16 – The Greek Post World War Order

"Beauty addresses itself chiefly to sight, but there is a beauty for the hearing too, as in certain combinations of words and in all kinds of music; for melodies and cadences are beautiful and minds that lift themselves above the realm of sense to a higher order are aware of beauty in the conduct of life, in actions, in character, in the pursuits of intellect; and there is the beauty of the virtues."

-Plotinus

In the immediate aftermath of the German withdrawal from Greece in 1944, the communist leftists initially had the upper hand and may well have taken hold of the entire nation if it was not for British intervention. Yes, Britain had long held Greece as a vital interest, and not wishing a communist takeover of the Greek homeland, the British decided to put their thumb on the scale in favor of the Greek nationalists.

In December of 1944, the Greek government in exile had returned, and with the support of the British, it was ready to do battle with the communist insurgency that had erupted in Greece. Of course, a major objective of this was to retake the capital of Athens. During the course of this conflict, over ten thousand people were killed, and much of the city was damaged. In the spring of 1945, the British brokered a provisional government led by Greek General Nikolaos Plastiras.

As a means of securing peace, Plastiras enacted a national amnesty, in which former communists were promised that they would not be prosecuted as long as they laid down their arms. But this declaration of amnesty never really materialized. Instead, the White Terror was unleashed against all who were even suspected of having anything to do with the communist forces. In this sweep for communists and communist sympathizers, thousands were thrown in jails and hundreds were killed, some of them for offenses so petty and obscure as simply uttering what was considered inflammatory rhetoric.

It seems that out of sheer fear, either of communists or of being labeled a communist, the traditional factions of Greek politics, the Venizelist-styled populist liberals and conservative royalists, joined forces at the ballot box. General elections were held in March of 1946, and a right-wing candidate named Constantine Tsaldaris (also known as Konstantinos Tsaldaris) came to power, fronting the United Patriotic Party. Tsaldaris continued the crackdown on suspected communist subversives. The situation became so oppressive that, by the summer of 1946, an estimated eighty thousand Greeks fled the country.

The following fall saw the return of King George II to Greece, although he would ultimately pass away just six months later, with his sibling Paul being crowned king in his place.

Despite the support of the monarchy in Greece and the persecution of the communists, many budding Marxists were waiting in the wings for a communist takeover. Much of their hope lay in the fact that the Soviet Union was increasing in power in the region. Among other things, Soviet leader Joseph Stalin had insisted that the British make their exit, and many believed that the vacuum that would be brought about with the withdrawal of the British might allow communist Marxists to come in and fill the gaps. The underground Communist Party of Greece, the KKE, even actively called for partisans to prepare themselves for the next phase of the armed struggle against the Greek state.

And then, on October 26th, 1946, Markos Vafeiadis marked a new milestone in the struggle by declaring that he had formed a new Democratic Army, which consisted of tens of thousands of fighters. Up until 1949, this group harassed and alluded Greek's state military by hiding out in remote tracts along the Yugoslavian and Albanian borders. The tactics this army employed were not dissimilar to how the Viet Cong hid in the borderlands between Cambodia, Laos, and Vietnam during the course of the Vietnam War.

For the rebels, relations with Yugoslavia were important since it was believed that Josip Broz Tito's communist regime might lend a hand to help. It was with this in mind that the KKE and its Democratic Army holed up in the mountains of Greece, waiting for the next fortuitous time to strike. That moment appeared in the spring of 1947 when the British announced to the United States that its position in Greece was no longer tenable.

But if the communists felt that the departure of the British would give them free reign in Greece, they had another thing coming. Shortly after the British announced their decision to withdraw, United States President Harry Truman announced his Truman Doctrine, which vowed that the United States was committed to "fight communism wherever it might appear in the world." This meant that the Greek communists were now up against one of the most powerful nations on the planet. Not only would the Americans send tons of money to right-wing Greek politicians, but it also would not hesitate to send boots on the ground if they thought it could deter a communist takeover.

The United States wanted to stand as a bulwark against communism, but the effect that US policy had with the more draconian measures being taken by the Greek government was certainly a little more than for which it had bargained. For after the United States essentially handed the Greek authoritarians a blank check, they basically went ballistic on the KKE.

Greece's infamous minister of public order, Napoleon Zerva, arranged the imprisonment of countless Greek dissidents. Civil liberties were also snuffed out when certain communist-leaning newspapers were banned, and then in December of 1947, the KKE itself was made illegal. All of these crackdowns, which had the West's backing, culminated in the declaration of martial law in 1948, during which hundreds were summarily executed on the spot.

These startling developments obviously caused the communists to change tactics, and the so-called "hardline Stalinist" of the KKE, Nikos Zachariadis, began to retool what was left of the Democratic Army. If anyone could survive an onslaught, it was Nikos Zachariadis. Nikos had actually been interned at the Dachau concentration camp for several years until he was liberated by the Allies. He then arrived back in Greece to his comrades in the spring of 1945 in what was a rather dramatic scene.

And during the martial law crackdowns of 1948, it was Nikos who positioned himself as being the one who could somehow snatch victory from the jaws of defeat. It was with this mindset that some twelve thousand communist fighters faced off against some seventy thousand federal Greek troops in what the Greek national government had dubbed "Operation Koronis."

The battle was waged in the borderlands between Greece and Albania, which was mountainous terrain. The communist rebels held out for several weeks, but after sustained pressure and even a NATO (North Atlantic Treaty Organization) bombing of Mount Grammos, they were ultimately left with two distinct choices: fight to the last man, or leave the country. Many chose the latter and fled across the border.

More trouble for the Greek communists emerged in July of 1948 when their fellow communist strongman Josip Broz Tito of Yugoslavia (better known simply as Tito) had a falling out with Stalin. The two would remain alienated for the rest of the Cold War. But the Greek Marxists now had to decide whether they should align with the isolated Tito, who was nearby, or the main wellspring of Marxism, the Soviet Union, which was farther to the north. Although Tito was a powerful neighbor, they opted to stick with the big guy in the north. It did not do them much good, though, since Stalin did not consider Greece strategically important enough for Soviet ambition to rile the Western powers.

And spurning Tito certainly did not do the revolutionaries any favors either since Tito promptly shut down his border with Greece, cutting off one of the main escape routes in the mountains. Those who did not get slaughtered by federal forces were forced to accept defeat, and many lived as exiles in Albania. Although the Cold War, which was between the forces of capitalism and communism, would continue for the better part of the 20th century, communism was rather decisively vanquished in Greece.

Greece proved to be the first great victory of the Western capitalists' efforts in stamping out communism. Greece, for its efforts, was rewarded with a seat at the NATO table. But even though Greece was given a solid role to play in the free world, Greek politics would remain polarized between far right and far left ideologies. Nevertheless, life in Greece dramatically improved between the early 1950s and early 1970s. This era, which is sometimes referred to as the Greek Miracle, saw Greece beset with such rapid economic advancement that the only country to outpace Greece's rapid ascent was Japan.

But even though the domestic situation was improving in Greece, there was still more than enough political discontent to muddy the waters. And that discontent came boiling to the surface in 1967 when members of the Greek armed forces managed to topple the duly elected prime minister, Panagiotis Kanellopoulos, in a military coup. This kick-started the rise of the Greek military junta, which would rule the country until 1974.

This military government was established by a couple of Greek colonels, namely, Georgios Papadopoulos, Nikolaos Makarezos, and Stylianos Pattakos. This takeover blindsided both the international community and many Greeks alike. The motivations for this junta were multiple, ranging from preventing a liberal party from solidifying power to ensuring that military officers received a long overdue pay raise.

But like with most authoritarian regimes, the fact that this group had seized power—regardless of the reasons—made them on the hook to maintain it. They knew that the second they relinquished the power that they had gained, they themselves would be held accountable. The junta lasted for nearly a decade, and it was largely continued by strongmen who found that once they held fast to the reins of power, they were simply unable to let go.

Once in power, the junta presented itself as the guardian of Greece. Predictably enough, the members of the junta were vehemently against communism. This allowed them to avoid the ire of the United States. However, this military clique was not well groomed enough to suit the traditional intelligentsia, and their ham-fisted ways most certainly did not get them into the good graces of the Greek elite.

They did their best to harness a sense of Greek nationalism by promoting what they viewed as the best of Greek history. In fact, the generals strove to rewrite the history books just to better promote their views. Having said that, some of their views were most certainly rather narrow-minded, such as the notion that men should not have long hair (this was during the late 1960s hippie heyday) and that women should not be allowed to wear mini-skirts.

But although some of the ultra-conservative sensibilities of the regime were somewhat jarring, the colonels managed to continue the steady rise of Greece's economy. They also made sure that the general standard of living went up. So, even if a man could not wear his hair long, most of the people were kept content due to the economy's progress. And whatever dissidents did emerge were quickly shut down. Criticism was stifled in the press, and anyone deemed to be against the government was hauled off to prison. It was in 1968/1969 that one of the greatest purges of dissidents occurred. Within this timeframe, several military officials, as well as a whopping nine hundred government officials, were sacked from their positions.

As the junta progressed, one colonel rose above the others— Colonel George Papadopoulos. The king of Greece more or less sat back in a state of helplessness while all of this was going on around him. The monarchy would finally come to an end when Papadopoulos moved to abolish it in June of 1973. He also went ahead and proclaimed that Greece was a republic with himself as president.

However, it would not last, and in just a matter of months, Papadopoulos was booted out of power and replaced by Colonel Dimitrios Ioannides. Colonel Ioannides was a true revolutionary, and he soon attempted to instigate upheaval in neighboring Cyprus. The status of Cyprus had long been a contentious issue between the Greeks and their neighbors, the Turks. At one time, Cyprus had been a part of the Byzantine Empire. The Turks had conquered it, and they controlled the region until the British took it from them in 1878. All throughout this period, Cyprus was heavily populated by Greeks, and in 1950, Archbishop Makarios III became the so-called "Ethnarch" of the island, which was a religious as well as a cultural leadership role over the Greek Cypriots. Makarios led a popular movement calling for unification with mainland Greece, which would dominate Greek political discussions over the next two decades.

Britain, in the meantime, began to push back against the notion, and great tensions were sparked as a result. The matter was then complicated when Turkish nationalists began to argue that Cyprus should become part of Turkey. This point was made clear in 1955 when, during a conference in London, it was proclaimed that the moment the British should leave the island, it would immediately return to the Turkish domain.

It was only when the Turks began to assert themselves over the island that the situation truly became dangerous. And the fact that both Turkey and Greece were NATO members made the situation all the more distressing for the Western powers.

In the meantime, Archbishop Makarios III had been officially elected president of Cyprus in December of 1959, cementing his role as the leader of the island. Earlier that year, the British had finally come around to the notion of the independence of Cyprus, and they reached an agreement with Cypriot authorities that would establish an autonomous Cypriot republic. These plans came to fruition in 1960 when a republic was officially declared.

Turkey, of course, was not too pleased with these developments, and soon, tensions were on the verge of boiling over. The colonels also had to deal with this problem. In fact, shortly after the colonels' military takeover of Greece, Turkey was threatening to invade the island in the wake of unrest between Greek and Turkish residents.

It was in light of all of this unrest that some began to consider an official union with Greece as a potential means of offsetting Turkish aggression in Cyprus. The colonels also sought to score some political points, thinking that laying claim to Cyprus was a surefire way to stir up Greek patriotism.

In June 1974, Greece's military-controlled government moved to support the union of Cyprus with Greece, thinking that by supporting a popular cause of the people, they would therefore ensure their own grip on power. However, relations with the military junta and the Makarios government on Cyprus were absolutely terrible at the time. Makarios presented himself as a centrist leader, and he had been at odds with the right-wing takeover of Greece from the beginning.

It was not long before Greece's military government began to hatch plots to get Makarios out of the way. These plans unraveled on July 15th, 1974, when Archbishop Makarios narrowly escaped an assassination attempt and ran to a British military base on Cyprus for help before being evacuated by helicopter. After Makarios's departure, Colonel Ioannides had a right-wing journalist by the name of Nikos Sampson installed in his place. Apparently, the Greeks in power hoped that Nikos could work with Greece to unite Cyprus to the motherland, but it was not to be. Before any such thing could happen, neighboring Turkey used the chaos as an excuse to invade Cyprus itself.

Turkey would dig in deep and occupy Northern Cyprus where a large Turkish population was already in place. This invasion would have ramifications that would last to this very day, with Cyprus becoming permanently divided between the so-called "Turkish Republic of Northern Cyprus" and the heavily Greek populated portion of southern Cyprus. The situation soon became so unstable, that Greece's military junta found itself unable to govern Greece—*let alone Cyprus.* And rather than riding on a wave of popular enthusiasm, it soon collapsed under its own weight.

Chapter 17 – Greece at the End of the Millennium

"The tyrant, who in order to hold his power, suppresses every superiority, does away with good men, forbids education and light, controls every movement of the citizens, and, keeping them under a perpetual servitude, wants them to grow accustomed to baseness and cowardice, has his spies everywhere to listen to what is said in the meetings, and spreads dissension and calumny among the citizens and impoverishes them, is obliged to make war in order to keep his subjects occupied and impose on them permanent need of a chief."

-Aristotle

After the military junta failed, the Third Hellenic Republic was declared in 1974, and Greek politician Konstantinos Karamanlis was made the interim prime minister on July 23rd, 1974. Although this was intended to just be a quick fix, Konstantinos was reelected for another two terms, along with his New Democratic Party.

Around this time, another powerful Greek political figure, Andreas Papandreou, made his way back to Greece and established a party known as PASOK. In English, PASOK basically stands for "Panhellenic Socialist Movement." Papandreou's party would continue to gain steam over the next few years, and it would ultimately become the driving force of Greece.

Konstantinos, in the meantime, would be elected once again in 1977, and his party gained 172 seats in the Greek Parliament. But it was Papandreou's party that was the real rising star, as it got a total of 25 percent of the vote that election, making it clearly the next most viable political party in Greece. Although Papandreou had eschewed anything to do with outright communism, he remained the choice for the socialist leftists, a fact that was proven when Papandreou won the presidency in 1981.

With Greek stability finally achieved, Greece entered into the growing European Union. Although Papandreou was a left-leaning socialist, he was at heart a populist since he channeled the popular sentiment of the Greek people at the time. And the most popular sentiment rising in the hearts of most Greeks was the sentiment of self-determination. Greece had been considered an independent state since 1821, but for many, this seemed to have been only an illusion, as Greece was constantly being buffeted by the intrigues of the surrounding great powers.

After all, at the dawning of Greek independence in 1821, European powers had felt that the Greeks were not ready for democracy, so they installed an autocratic king. Through this foreign-installed king, the Europeans continued to meddle in Greek internal affairs. Greece was made to fight in World War One at the behest of its European allies, and it was given the false impression that Greek-speaking regions of the defeated Ottoman Empire would be reincorporated into the Greek homeland.

Yet, when Turkey's Mustafa Kemal unleashed a ferocious onslaught against the Greeks, the Western powers did practically nothing to help. Greece had attempted to stay neutral during World War Two, but at the behest of Great Britain, it had been forced to allow British troops to enter its land, which led to a German invasion and occupation that the West was either too unprepared or too unwilling to prevent. After surviving the brutality of the Nazis, the Western powers continued to push Greece around, supporting right-wing governments out of fear of a communist takeover.

Many Greeks felt that this interference had led to the military junta and all of the turmoil that it brought. It was for all of this and more that the Greeks were inherently distrustful of the Western powers, even though the nation was a part of NATO and the European Union. It was also for this reason that Papandreou was so popular, as he spoke to the common man and insisted that he would help Greece stand on its own. Andreas Papandreou promised that Greece would determine its own destiny and would not get pushed around by outside forces anymore.

But as beloved as he was at home, his freethinking actions, which were often considered contrary to the Western consensus, caused him problems on the international stage. Papandreou was at odds with his international partners when, for example, he refused to condemn Libya for terrorist actions. This would have seemed like a common thing to do, at least for most of his partners, but Andreas Papandreou was not one who was ready to jump on the bandwagon of condemnation when incidents occurred. Even when Russia infamously shot down a Korean airliner, words of condemnation were not on Papandreou's lips.

And even though Greece was now part of the European Union (EU), rather than letting the EU force Greece into line, Andreas Papandreou turned the tables by thwarting EU objectives unless certain compromises were made to benefit Greece. Papandreou infamously blocked the entry of Portugal and Spain in the EU, and he used the Greek vote needed for their acceptance as a bargaining chip to get what he wanted.

Nevertheless, throughout the 1980s, Greece remained economically depressed. It is true that some living conditions improved. There was better healthcare, and some social safety nets were put in place to help the most unfortunate, but Greece would remain one of the poorest countries in Europe at the time. Papandreou won his reelection in 1985, but his party had lost a significant number of seats in the Greek Parliament. Then, as the economy worsened, Papandreou found himself having to push an "economic austerity package" through parliament.

This effort to curtail some of the excesses run up by the socialists led to fury from former Papandreou supporters, who began to openly riot in the streets in demonstrations in which some activists were killed. In an effort to pacify the growing discontent, PASOK attempted to reform certain areas of the economy and issue changes to the tax code. This led to one of the most controversial of PASOK's social engineering decisions. In April of 1987, the party decided to outright seize land owned by local churches. It was apparently figured that the best way to quiet down the landless peasants rioting in the streets would be to steal land from the church and divvy it up to them.

But none of their schemes worked as they had wanted. In fact, the situation only became worse. Soon, inflation was through the roof, and as currency crashed and grocery store prices skyrocketed, even generous government handouts of drachma meant absolutely nothing when the price of a loaf of bread suddenly cost more than anyone could possibly afford.

Papandreou, in the meantime, took a hit to his own personal popularity when he became embroiled in a scandalous affair with a former flight attendant by the name of Dimitra Liani. Andreas Papandreou left his wife Margaret and married Dimitra that year. It was with this dreadful backdrop that Papandreou ended his second term in the summer of 1989.

Out of this chaos, on November 22nd, 1989, a new coalition came together around perhaps an unlikely figure to lead the nation—an eighty-five-year-old former banker by the name of Xenophon Zolotas. The Zolotas government has been described as a "caretaker" administration, and it was put in place merely as a band-aid to prevent more hemorrhaging during the general political distress of the era. Soon, it became clear to the general public that Zolotas was not going to bring them what they wanted, which was better forms of employment and better economic conditions. Thus, there were once again massive protests in the streets and strikes being waged in the workplace.

Another election was then held in the spring of 1990, which brought forth a new coalition led by the New Democracy Party, which carried 150 seats in the Greek Parliament under the leadership of Constantine Mitsotakis (also known as Konstantinos Mitsotakis). With these staunch conservatives in power, Greece was steered away from its disastrous socialist programs of the past and into the direction of a full embrace of the free market. Soon, efforts were made to create the privatization of businesses, and there was a much more robust sense of competition in the economic sector. Social security programs, while left intact, were drastically curtailed in order to alleviate Greece's inflation, which at that time was the highest in Europe.

In the meantime, world politics were in the midst of a seismic shift due to the collapse of communism in eastern Europe, which was then followed by the end of communism in the Soviet Union itself. This collapse precipitated a massive influx of eastern European migrants passing through the Balkans to seek refuge in Greece. By early 1991, thousands of migrants had crossed into Greece from Albania alone. There was also a great migration of Russian Greeks from southern Russia and Ukraine who flowed into Greece proper, seeking to reunite with what they perceived as being their rightful ancestral homeland.

Waves of massive migration is a challenging issue for any country, especially when a nation is as economically depressed as Greece was at the time. Prime Minister Constantine Mitsotakis used a different tactic than his neutral, independent-minded predecessor and heartily embraced the European Union. He felt that the structures of the EU could do much to aid Greece's internal difficulties. Mitsotakis also slashed government spending and continued the privatization process of the previously state-run industrial sectors in an effort to finally get inflation under control.

Both of these efforts had their critics. There were those who were horrified at the sudden coziness with the EU, feeling that Greece was once again selling itself out to the European powers. And despite the obvious need to curtail inflation, for a public as dependent on socialist-styled programs as the Greeks were, suddenly taking those expensive programs away was not going to be an easy task.

As a result, Greek politics was more polarized than ever before. It was so polarized, in fact, that truth, lies, and even right and wrong all seemed to become secondary to "whose team" the Greeks were on. A perfect case in point of this occurred during the so-called "Bank of Crete scandal." The Bank of Crete was a major banking institution in Greece, which was rocked with a scandal when it was found that the bank had somehow "misplaced" hundreds of millions of dollars.

At the time, the chairman of the Bank of Crete was a rich Greek/American entrepreneur by the name of George Koskotas. Upon coming under investigation, Koskotas ultimately fled the country to escape prosecution. Koskotas was tied to PASOK and had deep links to the former prime minister, Andreas Papandreou. Koskotas, who was apprehended and placed in a Massachusetts prison, would later go on the record to state that bank audits that could have discovered the malfeasance were dismissed by members of PASOK and on at least two occasions by way of a telephone call from Andreas Papandreou himself. Not only that, Koskotas claimed that Papandreou used the Bank of Crete as his own personal piggy bank to finance political campaigns and events.

In the midst of all of these accusations, Papandreou had charges brought against him in 1992. What should have been a simple, clear-cut case of fraudulent financial activity was increasingly seen through two distinct political lenses by the populace. Rather than focusing on whether or not Papandreou was involved in money laundering, it seemed as if the political motivations behind the defense and prosecution were on trial. Left-wing supporters of Papandreou often agreed that Papandreou was guilty of the crimes with which he was charged but felt that his prosecution was wrong and being done out of sheer political spite. So even though they knew that he was most likely guilty of the crimes with which he was charged, these supporters belligerently clamored for a not guilty verdict.

Those who wished to see Papandreou found guilty were mostly using his financial malfeasance as a club with which to beat a man they found politically displeasing over the head. Not only that, the right wanted to use the indiscretions of Papandreou to castigate basically all who were associated with him. Thus, it was not just Papandreou who was on trial but also his whole political party. Such things are not too pretty, and often the long-term results for society are only increased polarization and discord.

In many ways, Papandreou was the fall guy used by his political opponents to destroy his entire political party. The public saw what was going on, and instead of focusing on simple matters of guilt or innocence, each side dug into their ideological corners and prepared for a long, drawn-out fight.

Papandreou was a rather astute politician, and he must have realized that his political support was his most valuable tool with which to bargain, and he used it. He welcomed the efforts of his political ideologues, and even with damning evidence against him, he steadfastly denied any wrongdoing and declared the whole effort to prosecute him as illegitimate. This must have been music to his base's ears, and they wholeheartedly agreed. Even without the advent of social media such as Facebook and Twitter, Papandreou managed to get the word out that he was fighting the charges, and his supporters rose up to stand by "their guy."

Papandreou, for all his faults, had an excellent political instinct, and as it turns out, his gut feelings were right. He did not think that the prosecution had the stomach to go all the way in their pursuit of justice, and in the spring of 1992, his intuition was confirmed when all charges were dropped. And not only did Papandreou beat the charges against him, he also went on to win the next round of elections, once again becoming prime minister of Greece in 1993.

Shocking their opponents, PASOK garnered roughly half of the vote and achieved a 170-seat majority in the Greek Parliament. And it was without question that the seventy-five-year-old icon of the left, Andreas Papandreou, would be selected to lead this new administration. Part of the reason behind this shocking win was the political and international climate at the time. Conflicts in the Balkan were erupting, and there was a real sense of insecurity among the Greek people.

To keep his base happy, Papandreou restarted some of the social programs that had been so popular in the past. He also curtailed much of the privatization of his predecessor, sticking to certain forms of centralization that Greece had grown accustomed to in the past. But one area in which Papandreou saw a dramatic shift was his change of heart about the European Union and the international community in general.

Faced with growing problems in neighboring regions such as the Balkans, Papandreou saw the EU as a solution rather than a problem. The overarching structure of the EU could help him make sense of the waves of eastern European migrants that had begun pouring across Greece's borders. He also began to believe that signing for a universal European currency could provide an answer to the failing drachma.

With the return of Papandreou, Greek polarization continued. And in what could only be seen as a political tit for tat, the previous prime minister, Constantine Mitsotakis, was suddenly hit with charges for supposedly profiting from illegal archeological excavations. This led to a trial being set for Mitsotakis in 1994, in which he faced these charges, as well as allegations of illegal wire taps and exploiting the privatization of a cement company, among other things. It seemed that there were political points to be made now that the ideological tide had changed. The elder Papandreou's health would give out before his political fortunes gave way, and in November of 1995, he ended up in the hospital with a bad case of pneumonia.

He would be in and out of the hospital, and his condition would only get worse. Finally, in January of 1996, Papandreou resigned, and he would ultimately pass away just months later. PASOK, in the meantime, found a viable successor in the form of one Constantine Simitis (better known as Costas or Kostas Simitis), and the party successfully won a majority in the fall of 1996. PASOK had staved off electoral defeat, but its members would have a wide variety of problems awaiting them as Greece counted down the last few years of the millennium.

First and foremost was the growing threat from the complete collapse of nearby Albania and Yugoslavia. A civil war in Bosnia proved to be the crisis that would draw in the world powers, and it would come dangerously close to provoking a larger regional conflict. The Greeks knew perhaps better than anyone else how much of a powder keg the Balkans really were. After all, one world war had been sparked in the Balkans, and it would not be too hard to imagine another being sparked in this contentious region.

The Greeks did not want to be pulled into a conflict, so they did everything they could to stay neutral while simultaneously attempting to assuage the situation. Greece kept up a dialogue with Belgrade while strategizing with the Russians about the best to way to get the outside powers to go a little easier on the Bosnian Serbs. In 1995, NATO led bombing campaigns against areas held by the Bosnian Serbs. And as much as Greece wanted to maintain its neutrality, Greek officials went on the record to criticize the bombing.

Fortunately for the Greeks, NATO soon called for a ceasefire, which means that Greece would not be forced to take any action that might threaten its neutrality. Greece did agree to send some Greek troops to the region shortly thereafter, not to fight but as part of a peacekeeping mission. Greece also officially set up diplomatic contact with officials in Bosnia.

However, this would not be the end of the turmoil in the Balkans. In 1998, tensions in the Yugoslavian region of Kosovo erupted in bloodshed. Soon, it seemed that Greece would once again be flooded with countless refugees from the Balkans. NATO then began conducting new rounds of airstrikes in the region, and Greece found itself once again struggling to find its footing.

Many Greeks supported the Christian Serbs and were upset with what they perceived as foreign meddling by NATO. This sentiment was on full display when United States President Bill Clinton came to Athens in 1999. He was thronged by Greek protesters wherever he went. Clinton was there to shore up the support of Greece since it was a fellow NATO member, but he found himself having to become an apologist for all of the previous perceived missteps of NATO in the past.

However, Clinton did manage to gain a few concessions in his discussions with Greek officials. Greece would allow NATO forces to station themselves in Greece, although it was insisted that the Greeks themselves would take no part in any military engagements.

After these international crises in the Balkans had subsided, Greece was able to focus on the even more pressing matters of a failing economy. Knowing that the drachma was beyond redemption, Greece began to pin its hopes on the euro of the

European Union. And at the dawning of the new millennium, Greece had officially made the euro its official form of currency, doing so by 2001.

Chapter 18 – Modern Day Greece (2001-2021)

"Unfortunately, corruption is widespread in government agencies and public enterprises. Our political system promotes nepotism and wasting money. This has undermined our legal system and confidence in the functioning of the state. One of the consequences is that many citizens don't pay their taxes."."

-George Papandreou

The year 2001 started out as a happy one for the Greeks. The economic situation seemed to be on the mend with the advent of the euro, and Greece's international state of affairs seemed to be at peace. That May, even the visit of Pope John Paul II emerged as a sign of great reconciliation between Greece and the world since it was the first time a Catholic pope had been to Orthodox Greece in around 1,290 years.

During his stop, the pope actually apologized to the Greeks for the historic antagonism of the Catholic Church against the Greek Orthodox faithful. He even apologized for the Catholic Crusaders from the West who had sacked Constantinople in 1204 on their way to fight in the Middle East. The pope spoke in Athens, saying, "Clearly there is a need for a liberating process of purification of memory. For the occasions past and present, when sons and daughters of the Catholic Church have sinned by actions and omission against their Orthodox brothers and sisters, may the Lord grant us the forgiveness we beg of him."

In what seemed to be a repeat of the massive protests against Bill Clinton in 1999, the pope, too, was greeted with throngs of protesters. Some of these shouted a litany of anti-pope slogans in which the pontiff was dubbed an "arch-heretic" and even "the grotesque, two-horned monster of Rome." But despite all of the noise, the pope's trip was deemed to have been an overall success.

Along with apologizing for the past misdeeds of the Catholic Church, the pope spoke of how the Orthodox Church, due to its close proximity to Islamic lands, was situated on the very frontiers of Christianity. Greece had indeed kept a wary eye toward any sign of Muslim extremism rising up among its Middle Eastern neighbors. Cyprus, of course, was still an incredibly contentious issue between Greece and Turkey, and this flashpoint could have created an uncontrollable conflagration.

However, it was not a threat from regional Islamic power players that would gain the attention of Greece's foreign policy advisors in the fall of 2001. Greece, like much of the rest of the world, would be stunned on the morning of September 11th, 2001, to learn of a catastrophic terrorist attack launched against the United States. In one day, a group of radicalized Muslim extremists, working at the behest of terror mastermind Osama bin Laden, had killed nearly three thousand Americans.

In the aftermath of this brazen attack, the United States received an outpouring of both condolences and offers of support from a multitude of heads of state. Among them was Greek Prime Minister Costas Simitis, who proclaimed, "Greece condemns, most categorically, these horrific acts. We hope that the culprits be located and brought to justice immediately." The culprits were the Saudi-based terror group Al-Qaeda, whose headquarters at the time was in the remote reaches of Afghanistan. The same mountainous and unruly Afghanistan that Alexander the Great had attempted to tame for the Greeks thousands of years before (Alexander founded Kandahar) was now ground zero for the opening stages of the war on terror.

Greece, acting as a NATO member, sent Greek troops to fight alongside Americans in an operation that the United States military termed "Operation Enduring Freedom." The fight was against not only Al-Qaeda but also the Afghan warlords of the Taliban who had sheltered them. The mission was successful in the short term in the sense that it rooted out Al-Qaeda (most fled to the Pakistan border) and severely degraded the Taliban. But the long-term effects are still being debated to this very day.

Overall, the Greek presence was a minimal one, with the first batch of 150 soldiers arriving in January of 2002. The war effort quickly lost popular support among many in Greece, and by 2004, Greek politicians were actively calling for the withdrawal of all Greek forces in the region.

This same year, Greece hosted the Olympics. This was a big deal for Greece. Since the land of Greece was the home of the original Olympics, Athens, of course, wanted to outshine all of the others. As such, Greece spent a lot of money hosting the Olympic Games, far more than it probably should have (in total, it spent nine billion US dollars).

However, just a few years into its entrance into the eurozone (the union of European states that use the euro), Greece was riding high on new economic opportunities and went on a spending spree. All of this spending would come back to haunt them when Greece was hit with the global economic recession of 2007/2008.

The root causes of this global economic downturn, otherwise known as the Great Recession, are fairly complex. A main triggering factor was the bursting of the so-called "housing bubble" in the United States. For many years in the United States, housing prices were steadily rising. It was a sellers' market, but starting in 2007, house prices began to fall dramatically. Many homes were foreclosed upon, and as a result, the banks that backed these properties lost money. When the banks in America began to go bankrupt in rapid numbers, it created a ripple effect that was felt all across the world.

Back in Greece, in the meantime, elections in the fall of 2009 saw the return of PASOK. After PASOK came to power, the Greek minister of finance informed the EU's European Commission that Greece's debt would skyrocket to 12.5 percent of its gross domestic product (GDP), which was over twice of what the prior administration had reported. If this was not alarming enough, further investigation revealed that the situation was even worse than that and that the true figure was closer to 15.4 percent.

The European Union requires all members to produce accurate economic data within the eurozone, and the backlash against Greece was swift and fierce. Other member states of the EU were absolutely appalled at what appeared to be outright falsification of records by corrupt Greek officials. In the aftermath of this loss of trust, Greece's credit rating plummeted, which meant that Greece would now be subject to much higher interest rates. It would later be figured out that Greek politicians had been cooking the books for quite some time and had even given false data to ease its entrance into the eurozone itself.

In the immediate aftermath of Greece's economic collapse, austerity measures were imposed to try and get the Greek economy afloat. This meant that Greece's government would have to scale back spending while funneling more money out of the Greek people through increased taxation. These harsh measures led the International Monetary Fund (IMF) to agree to loan Greece 110 billion euros in 2010. Although not a complete bailout, this money did allow the struggling country to at least pay interest on its current debt so that it could be kept from going into complete default and being forced to leave the eurozone altogether.

The following year, in 2011, the European Financial Stability Facility generously deposited another 190 billion euros to the aid that had already been dished out to Greece. It was also agreed that half of all money Greece owed to private creditors would be blotted out. This made the servicing of Greece's still existing debt much easier to manage.

By 2014, the Greek economy appeared to be on the rebound, with a growth rate of 0.7 percent. That same year, Greece was allowed to come back to the international bond market. But despite these gains, over the next few years, Greece would continue to nearly default while having to borrow additional funds just to stay afloat. Greece had its final bailout in August of 2018, receiving a total of 290 billion euros over the years. As of this writing, Greece is expected to continue to make payments on its debts all the way until August of 2060.

Conclusion: Hellenism at the Crossroads

Greece was a land of many firsts. It was here that democracy, theater, and the Olympics first came to prominence. The ideals of Hellenism quickly spread far and wide. This spark of Greek ingenuity would survive the conquest of foreign powers and even go on to fuel the European Renaissance. Greece then finally gained its national independence in 1821, and the future of the Greek-speaking world seemed promising once again.

Two centuries later, in 2021, Greece was facing some pretty significant challenges. Along with its continuing efforts to get out of debt, Greece, like much the rest of the world, had been rocked by a global pandemic. Greece has been largely credited with doing a good job of handling the pandemic, but the impact of recent events continues to present a challenge.

The fact that tourism was largely shut down in the spring and summer of 2020 was a definite setback for Greece's economy since tourism makes up about 20 percent of Greece's total GDP. However, Greece is a resilient nation, and it seems like when the chips are down, the Greeks tend to be at their best. Greece was among the countries who took a leading role in vaccinations and made sure that all of those who worked in tourism were fully vaccinated.

Greece has fought off ferocious foes in the past, and the pandemic has been viewed as just the latest beast for the Greeks to subdue. The Greeks are willing to overcome this obstacle just like all the others they have faced throughout their long and rich history. Right now, Hellenism may seem to be at the crossroads, but the world can most certainly expect many more new and exciting epochs of Greek culture to come.

Free Bonus from Captivating History (Available for a Limited time)

Hi History Lovers!

Now you have a chance to join our exclusive history list so you can get your first history ebook for free as well as discounts and a potential to get more history books for free! Simply visit the link below to join.

Captivatinghistory.com/ebook

Also, make sure to follow us on Facebook, Twitter and Youtube by searching for Captivating History.

Here's another book by Captivating History that you might like

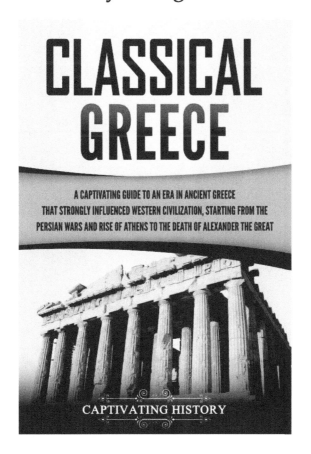

Made in the USA
Middletown, DE
28 June 2023

33978869R00096